HOW TO USE YOUR LAW DEGREE

Law Degree and No Job? No Problem.

17 ways to begin practicing NOW, Regardless of the job market.

Jeanne M. Hepler

This book is dedicated to my law partner Michael McHale Collins, who taught me much of what I know, and to my daughter Jess Lassere Ryland, who is finding her own path in the practice of law.

CONTENTS

INTRODUCTION

A law degree can be used to make a good living. You just have to know how.

Got any good lawyer jokes? Here's one, "What do you call a law school graduate?"
Sadly,   the   answer   is   increasingly   becoming: "Unemployed."

SOURCE: HUFFINGTON POST ARTICLE
HTTP://WWW.HUFFINGTONPOST.COM/NATALIE-GREGG/MAMAS-DONT-LET-YOUR-BABIE_2_B_6457898.HTML.

This is a book about how to start practicing law, with little or no experience. I wrote this book for those of you who graduated from law school and can't find a job. It is also for those law school graduates who found a job, but don't like what they're doing and want to make a change. It will especially help those of you who are boldly wishing to start your own practices and are not sure where to begin.

Think of this book as an opportunity to pick the brain of a lawyer with over thirty years of experience in general practice, brainstorming about what areas of law could be undertaken by someone with little or no experience, and how to go about it. I will talk about 17 different areas of practice which I believe could be entered by a lawyer with little or no experience, and for each one, tell you what the practice involves, what kind of fees to expect, what the practice looks like on a day to day basis (I'll walk you through the basic mechanics of an average case), what type of lawyer might be a good fit for that practice, how to go about acquiring the necessary skills, and how to find clients and build the practice.

Why did I write this book? I have been practicing law for over thirty years, mostly as a general practitioner. I am at the point now where I am enjoying a mature practice and am considering retirement. It occurs to me that I have amassed a wealth of knowledge and experience, and it seems a shame to just let that dissipate into the ether when I retire.

I have read much about the plight of recent law school graduates. It's hard to find a job. The market is tough out there. Lots of new lawyers are not able to use their law degrees, because they can't find employment as a lawyer. It is a lousy feeling, having worked so hard and done everything right, only to end up with a huge student loan debt and no job. Or, if you are lucky enough to have found a job, you might find yourself in an associate mill, where you grind out the billable hours night and day until you're exhausted and burned out.

A law degree can be a very valuable asset. The trick is to learn how to use it and turn it into cash, and there are numerous ways to do that. Every day, I am grateful that I am able to receive a handsome fee in exchange for my knowledge and experience, and my law degree made that possible. Those of you reading this book are probably facing the chasm between the law degree and the necessary knowledge and experience. I hope that this book helps you begin to build a bridge over that chasm and turn your law degree into a valuable asset instead of just a very expensive piece of paper.

Law school does not do a great job of preparing you for the real world. When I graduated from law school in 1985, I had lots of book knowledge about torts and contracts and criminal conspiracy and easements and maritime law, but I had no idea what a lawsuit looked like, or how to file one. I've heard that things have improved, and law schools now do a better job of preparing students to actually practice law. But still, some things have to be learned on the job. It can feel overwhelming to sit there with your law degree in hand, with no idea how to begin being a lawyer. That's why I wrote this book.

For those of you who might be feeling that you're not lawyer material, that law school was a big mistake, that you hate public speaking, you can't stand controversy, and you don't know what you were thinking going to law school in the first place, take heart. That's how I felt, for a long time. I can tell you now, from the other end of the timeline, that there are plenty of niches for you in law. There are endless opportunities to help people, with or without court, and plenty of ways to feed your inner nerd. This book will give you several options.

This book is not a magic bullet. You won't have a full-time practice by next month. But the important thing is to get started, and I will tell you exactly how to take those first few steps, and give you a blueprint for moving forward, so that you will actually be using your degree and gaining experience. Don't get caught up in the details or feel like you need to know exactly how this is all going to turn out. You won't know. Think of your career as a growing, living thing that will take its own unique shape over time. You can try to imagine its final shape now, but you will probably be wrong. You will acquire new information along the way, changing course here and there, you will make contacts and be offered opportunities, such as employment, shared office space, or client referrals. There is simply no way to predict where you will end up. Nurture your career by continuing to learn and move forward, and watch for opportunities along the way, and your path will open up before you in ways that you never expected.

If you had told me thirty years ago that I'd be the managing partner of a thriving firm, with a talented and wonderful law partner and three awesome associates, I'd never have believed you. If you had told me that I would one day fight hard in court against scary experienced lawyers and win, I'd have thought you definitely had the wrong person. But those things happened, just by taking one step at a time, and trying all the while to find what felt right for me. Baby steps add up to big things. What looks overwhelming to you now will someday look simple. The trick is to get started and take the first step.

"Until one is committed, there is hesitancy, the chance to draw back. Concerning all acts of initiative (and creation), there is one elementary truth, the ignorance of which kills countless ideas and splendid plans: that the moment one definitely commits oneself, then Providence moves too. All sorts of things occur to help one that would never otherwise have occurred. A whole stream of events issues from the decision, raising in one's favor all manner of unforeseen incidents and meetings and material

assistance, which no man could have dreamed would have come his way. **Whatever you can do, or dream you can do, begin it. Boldness has genius, power, and magic in it.** *Begin it now."*

(This quote is usually attributed to Goethe, although, if you're a stickler for details, some say it was maybe just inspired by Goethe: http://german.about.com/library/blgermyth12.htm)

I know it sounds corny, but the sky is the limit. Actually, the real limits are usually those that you place on yourself when you believe that you can't do something. (This is called a self-limiting belief – it's a "thing" in psychology.) You can do this. I don't know you, but if you were smart enough to finish law school, I know you can do this. Don't let you tell yourself otherwise.

Even if you're not interested in building your own practice, any experience actually practicing law will put you way ahead in terms of being more attractive to potential employers down the road. An inexperienced law school graduate is a money loser for most small law firms, because it takes so long to train a new lawyer how to practice law and be productive. The more experience you bring to the table, the more hirable you become. And if you actually bring your own clients to the table as well as experience, even better!

In this book, I will tell you what you need to do, what each type of practice will look like, and how to get started. What I won't tell you is exactly what is required in your particular state. I practice in Virginia. States vary considerably, and I freely admit this throughout the book. However, much of the basics are the same everywhere, and I give you a heads up on the areas that I feel will vary considerably from state to state. I tell you where to go to find the specifics in your own state. Again, the basics should remain fairly consistent throughout the states, and the book is definitely worthwhile overall, even without being a state-by-state treatise, and even if some of the practice areas work differently in your state. If I had to research all 50 states for all 15 areas of practice and give you a blow by blow on how each state works, that would have been overwhelming, and I simply would not have done it.

Please know that this book is only a guideline based on my experience in Virginia. I make no guarantees, and I urge you to check the laws in your jurisdiction before you undertake any legal practice.

I am happy with this book, and feel that it is worthwhile, and I sincerely hope that it helps you and motivates you to get started. I wish that I had had this when I started out. I hope that this book gives you a blueprint to find the confidence to strike out on your own and start practicing law – you know, that thing that you paid all that money to be able to do? And three years of hard work? Use that degree! You earned it. Here's how.

THE BASICS

BASIC REQUIREMENTS

This book assumes that you have a law degree, and have either passed the bar, or intend to do so. (If the bar has been a problem for you, don't close this book yet. I have ideas for work you can do without passing the bar. See sections on Appellate Work, Freelance Contract Lawyer, Real Estate Title Searcher, and Social Security Disability.)

You will also need a computer, scanner (I love the Fujitsu Scansnap, which comes with Adobe Acrobat software), a printer that is not too expensive ink cartridge-wise (we use the HP Officejet pro, which is inexpensive and fast, but does not print color – we have another printer we use for color brochures, etc.), and phone (a cell phone is fine), as well as the internet and some ability to do legal research (either on free online sites or with a purchased service, or access to a law library or attorney's office that will let you use theirs). You should be able to use your computer, and draft documents with ease. (If you don't pass this test, get thee to a computer course immediately.) You should eventually get business cards, and they don't have to be expensive. (Later, when you want to "brand" your practice as being more high end, or raise your fees, you will want really nice cards.) You will need stationery (white copy paper and white envelopes are fine, with a simple letterhead that you can design and save as a form). You will probably need some stamps. You need something professional-looking to schlep your stuff around in, like a briefcase, or, if you're going cheap, a pack of accordion folders will do just fine. You will also want the basic office supplies: stapler and staples, staple remover, tape, paper clips, pens, post-it notes.

You will also need Errors and Omissions (E&O) Insurance, or legal malpractice insurance. Google around to find carriers serving your locality, and also check with your state bar to find out which providers they recommend. I have no idea what it will cost you to become insured (and it will depend on your chosen limits of coverage, etc.), but I'm guessing somewhere between $1,000 and $5,000 for your first year. Hopefully, they will let you get on a payment plan. Note: this is where going into partnership with other new lawyers can save money, as it will cost less to cover the partnership than it would cost to cover the individual partners. If you can't swing the E&O Insurance, you will have to find work under someone's else's policy, as a part time, full time, or flex time employee of another lawyer or law firm.

Anyone going to court will need a good suit or other courtroom attire. Actually, anyone who is quoting a fee to a client (or another lawyer) should be wearing something crisp and professional. The higher the fee, the more sharply you should be dressed. Like it or not, your appearance informs not only the client, but yourself (subconsciously) of your worth.

To summarize, you will need:

o   Law degree and pass the bar (or plan to pass the bar soon).
o   Computer (that you know how to use), scanner, and printer.
o   A way to do legal research.
o   A cell phone.
o   Stationery (white copy paper and envelopes), and postage stamps.
o   Office supplies: stapler and staples, staple remover, tape, paper clips, pens, post-it notes.
o   A briefcase, or a supply of accordion folders.
o   Professional attire.
o   E&O Insurance.
o   Business cards, once you know what your business will be.

OFFICE SPACE

Most areas of practice I cover will require a place to meet with the client, but some types of work can easily be done from home or started from a home office. Refer to the subsection titled "Practice From Home?" under each area of practice I cover, to see my recommendations.

If you need space to meet with clients, and you can't afford the overhead of permanent office space, you will have to get creative.

If you are in a larger metropolitan area, there may be office spaces that can be rented by the hour. Depending on your practice, you may still need to find a notary and witnesses, for example, if your client is signing a Will. Some states, such as Kentucky, allow you, the lawyer, to act as the notary, while others do not permit it. You will need to check your state statutes to find out.

Your local courthouse may have rooms available for lawyers to meet with clients or witnesses. These may be on a first come, first served basis, or you may be able to reserve them.

Another option would be to arrange to occasionally use space in the office of an attorney who does not practice your area of law but may be able to co-counsel with you or refer clients to you, such as a general practitioner. A lawyer who has a totally unrelated practice may also be happy to "rent" office space to you on an as-needed basis and could provide access to their notary public as well.

If an as-needed office-sharing arrangement works out long-term, you may be able to eventually share office space on a full-time basis, which would decrease overhead for both of you, especially if you form a partnership or professional corporation or limited liability company and share the cost of malpractice insurance and staff. There is no reason to co-mingle your income unless you both decide you want to, but if you form a partnership or PC or PLLC, you will need to hire an accountant to work out the numbers at the end of the year, to allocate the right amount of total business income (and overhead) to each of you. You should also draft a business agreement to outline your understanding. But that's down the line.

All you need right now is to rent office space as needed, with the ability to use the attorney's notary public if your practice requires that.

You may also find a lawyer who has an extra office that you can rent full time for a nominal fee, and they may even be willing to provide phone service or secretarial service for another fee. You might even get creative and call yourself an employee so that you can be on their E&O policy, if you can structure your financial arrangement to help cover that cost. (Usually the E&O insurance premium does not automatically go up if a firm adds a lawyer, but when the policy renews, the premium will be adjusted at that time to reflect the additional lawyer.)

Another route is to go into partnership with one or more other lawyers like yourself who want to start their own practices but need to share overhead costs. You don't need to practice in the same area, and in fact, can refer clients to each other if you don't.

You may also have a spouse, friend, or family member with an office (it doesn't have to be a law office, although obviously that would be ideal) who can let you use space there, or rent you space there, when they are not using it.

If all else fails, you can meet with clients at their own homes. If you are doing estate planning, this may be comfortable, but if you are doing criminal defense, it may not always feel safe or even, at times, sanitary.

You could also meet with clients at your home office, if you are able to put together a confidential and professional-feeling space within your home.

Whenever you have a home office, whether it is where you meet with clients or not, you can deduct home office expenses for tax purposes.

THE ENTITY

I f you will be practicing law (as opposed to performing work that can be done by a non-lawyer), you should create a professional limited liability company before you start. It's easy to do, it's not expensive, and it will help protect you from personal liability. Just Google how to form a professional limited liability company in your state, and there may even be a form online that you just have to fill out and send to your state's State Corporation Commission with a check for $100 or so. Check your state laws to be sure you are doing all you need to do. In the alternative, if you prefer, you can form a professional corporation. There may be tax advantages for one over the other, which you could discuss with your accountant. Or you could just keep it simple and go with the PLLC.

Decide on a name for yourself. It can be Your Name, PLC. Or you can get creative and give yourself a descriptive name, such as Traffic Matters, PLC. Before you do that, though, check with your state bar and see if that type of fictitious name is allowed in your state. Before you decide on a firm name, be sure to check to see if that domain name is available. You can find out easily at Godaddy.com. If you can't get the domain name, choose another name, for example Your Name Law, PLC, or whatever you can get the domain name for. It costs less than ten dollars a year to own the domain name.

WEBSITES

Most areas of practice will require a website. Refer to each chapter regarding the importance of a website for each different type of practice.

Go to GoDaddy, or a similar service, and secure your firm's domain name. (JohnSmithPLC or TrafficMattersPLC or whatever). If the domain name is unavailable, you will have to choose a different name for your firm.

You need a logo of some sort, even if it is just your name in a certain font. This can be designed in conjunction with your website (by using a website template) or you can try doing it yourself or hire someone to do it for you. Know anyone with an art degree? Depending on how comfortable you are with designing your own site, you may want to consider hiring a website designer to get you started, although you can definitely work up a very nice site using GoDaddy or Weebly, adding pictures in from an online source such as Fotilia.

Once you have your domain name, decide how you are going to create your website. If you are not sure what to do, just go to Weebly and see if you can develop one yourself. Weebly will cost a minimal amount per month, as will GoDaddy. Weebly has a free option, but you should choose one of the payment plans, or your website will not look professional (it will be a Weebly.com site instead of your own domain).

Your site should have a menu bar at the top of the page that lists pages such as "Home," "About Us," "Contact," "Attorneys," "Practice Areas," etc. You can also have a page named "Resources" with handy links, such as links to an online breath alcohol calculator, if you do traffic defense, or a link to an Alzheimer's support group, if you do elder law. Your menu bar can also have a link to your blog.

After you have a few satisfied clients, you should start listing Testimonials on your website.

It is a good idea to have a blog. Try to write something at least once a month. It doesn't have to be scholarly, or a work of art. Just some interesting tidbit of information will do. Try to include words that will appear in the types of searches people will do to find you, such as "speeding ticket" if you are a traffic lawyer, or "nursing home" if you do elder law. Regular posting will boost SEO (Search Engine Optimization), as will the use of key search words in your postings. Posting a video of yourself giving basic advice on your area of practice can also be good for SEO.

Post a picture of yourself on your website. It puts people at ease to see who they will be dealing with.

It's not a bad idea to have a Contact form which allows potential clients to email you with inquiries. Be sure to include nearby a disclaimer stating that no attorney-client relationship will be created simply by the inquiry, and that no confidential information should be shared therein.

Check your state bar regulations to be sure your website is in compliance with local rules on attorney advertising. Don't be afraid to ask your state bar committee on ethics to review your website and give you feedback for compliance. That is part of the service they provide, and they are generally very nice about it, at least in my state of Virginia. Often, the requirements are quite specific, and easy to comply with by making minor changes to font size, page placement, or language.

An easy way to be able to accept credit card or debit card payments is by adding a Paypal link to your website. This is especially helpful for traffic defense cases, when a lot of your clients may be just passing through your jurisdiction and don't live nearby. You can also use a service such as Square.

If you decide to take credit card or debit payments by a service such as Square, or if you take Paypal payments, be sure to set up the system so that your fee for the service is taken out of your general operating account, rather than your escrow account. The client's retainer or fee can either go into your general account, then be moved immediately to escrow until earned, or, preferably, be deposited directly into escrow, but the Square fee or Paypal fee that you pay for the service should not come out of escrow. If you can't figure out how to get the service fee taken from your operating account while the retainer or client fee goes into escrow, then have the fee deposited into the operating account, then transfer the entire retainer or client fee into general, then deposit the original amount of the retainer or client fee into escrow, NOT the net fee after your service fee to Square or Paypal is deducted. Picky, I know. But that's how you should do it, at least in Virginia, where it is improper to have the service charge taken out of the client fee. Square or Paypal may be able to help you set it up properly in the beginning, with the gross retainer or client fee going into escrow, and the service fee being automatically deducted from your operating account, rather than being deducted from the client retainer or fee.

BANK ACCOUNTS

You will need two bank accounts, or three, if you do real estate closings. Note, however, that I do not cover real estate closings as one of my 17 areas of practice. Although they are easy to do, they have become highly regulated, and I have chosen not to include them in this book. In some states, however, they can be done by non-lawyers, so they may be an option for those of you who have had trouble passing the bar. The bank accounts you will need are:

1. A general account, into which you deposit your income, and from which you pay your bills and your own salary (and that of any employees). You will also use this account to pay any reimbursable expenses related to cases.
2. An escrow account, into which you place your retainers and fees until you have earned them, at which time you transfer the earned fee into the general account. NEVER screw with your escrow account, unless you want to find yourself before an ethics committee. That's not your money. It's your clients' money, until you earn it and put it in your general account.
3. If you conduct real estate closings, you will also need a CRESPA account, which is an escrow account that holds real estate closing money and is highly regulated. Never, ever screw with that one. Closing money goes in, and all money going out is tracked in minute detail. None of it is yours, except the check you write to yourself for your closing fees.

You can have a fourth account, if you wish to transfer money into savings, or if you want to keep a separate payroll account (you won't need a separate payroll account unless and until you have some employees).

COMPUTER SOFTWARE

I am not a Mac user (and yes, I wish I were). Our office uses Microsoft Office 365. All you really need is Word (for word processing) and Outlook (for emails and calendars). Excel and Powerpoint can also come in handy.

Make use of Cloud storage if you can. At this writing, Sharepoint and Dropbox are two good options. Dropbox is easier to set up and use if you're not a computer geek. If you don't have cloud storage, you will need to be diligent about confidential storage and backups of your data. You would hate to lose everything if your computer suddenly died or was stolen. I strongly recommend that you hire an IT consultant to advise you regarding secure cloud storage, as confidentiality is of utmost importance.

You will have to do your own bookkeeping, so consider Quickbooks at some point, but you can, and should, certainly start out keeping books on paper. Using Quickbooks with escrow accounts is a mind-bending challenge that will (believe me) require the assistance of a Quickbooks expert, and NOT the ones that work for Quickbooks technical assistance – in my experience they have no idea how to set up and use escrow accounts in Quickbooks, although they will cheerfully say they do and lead you in the wrong direction for months on end until you have to scrap the whole thing and find someone who really knows how to do it. I found my expert on a Quickbooks forum, where she was answering technical questions online. She was in another state, but was able to easily help us remotely.

Office management software: Unless you develop a 50 lawyer firm, you won't need it. Keep it simple and stick with the Microsoft products. (Sorry, Mac users, I'm no help to you). Less is more right now. Tony Robbins has wisely pointed out that "Complexity is the Enemy of Execution." However, if you really want to use office management software and you have the money, MyCase and Amicus Attorney are said to be some of the best for small firms. Some folks love them - I have tried both of them and am happier just using Microsoft Office and Quickbooks.

LIBRARY AND FORMS

B esides your legal research program, you will need whatever publications and forms are required for you to get up to speed and be prepared to practice in your chosen area. Refer to each chapter for an idea of what you will need.

OPTIONAL SUPPLIES FOR LITIGATORS

If your state publishes a Judge's Deskbook, buy one or try to get your hands on one, if you'll be doing any litigation. (See if the local bar has a law library and look to see what books it contains.) In Virginia, there is a Judge's Deskbook for Circuit Court (upper court), and a Judge's Deskbook for General District Court (lower court). These are invaluable. They are designed to be an easy reference for judges to use when they are unsure of the law. For instance, what are the exceptions to the hearsay rule? When can a police officer stop a car? Those kinds of answers are at your fingertips in these deskbooks.

If your state or your Continuing Education providers publish an evidence handbook, I'd advise getting one for anyone going near a courtroom. Virginia has an excellent one, and it even comes in digital format. Keep this with you in court for those times when you are just stumped and don't know the evidentiary rule at hand. It can save your skin. You will also refer to it often when preparing for trial.

In Virginia, there is a two-volume set of civil jury instructions and a two volume set of criminal jury instructions that have been approved by the courts. You can buy them. I'm sure it's similar in your state. As long as you are using the approved instructions, you are golden. Actually, it's a great practice to look at the jury instructions early in the case, when you are involved in jury trial litigation, because they will tell you exactly what you will need to prove.

MARKETING SUPPLIES

Brochures and Flyers. For some areas of practice, I recommend that you design, write, and print brochures or flyers for marketing purposes. You can make and print them at home, or you can make very professional products using online services such as Vistaprint and photographs from an online source such as Fotolia or Wikimedia Commons. You will look like an instant expert with color brochures discussing your area of practice, and they don't take that long to put together. Remember that (most of the time) you're writing for laypersons, not other lawyers. Keep the language simple and easy to understand.

Logo. You may want to have a logo for your business, to be printed on the cards, brochures and flyers. See my chapter on Websites.

If you intend to do a lot of public speaking for marketing purposes, you may want to consider buying a projector and portable screen, and at some point maybe a laser pointer and a microphone to project your voice.

If you intend to participate in any marketing events where you will be expected to set up a table, consider purchasing a custom tablecloth and banner, or all the other tables will make you look sad and shabby (I found this out the hard way). You will also want brochures, business cards, and maybe even some gifts like pens, magnets, or even just a bowl of candy. Otherwise, no one will stop at your table. You can get the tablecloth and banner online, as well as pens, magnets, and lots of other swag. Again, you may want to have a logo for your business, to be printed on the tablecloth, banner, and swag.

SETTING UP YOUR SYSTEMS

Under each area of practice I give ideas on where and how to find the forms you will need for the practice, and how to obtain the information necessary to create checklists.

Since you're just starting out, develop good habits early. You should have a written retainer agreement with each client, setting out the scope of what you have agreed to do, and the fee agreement. It's helpful if the retainer agreement states exactly when you are entitled to take your fee (for example, when all documents are drafted, or when the hearing is completed, etc., depending on the case).

You should also have a closing letter form ready to send when the case is over. Consider including in the closing letter a request for a testimonial, and/or direct the client to AVVO, Lawyers.com, etc. and ask them to rate your services. Consider omitting this request if you and the client didn't get along.

Checklists are a great way to avoid trouble. I strongly recommend having a checklist for your type of practice, laying out all the usual steps in your process. When you're new at your work, this will be a lifesaver. When you get busy with a lot of clients, this will be a lifesaver. It will also allow you to easily delegate certain items to an assistant later, which will be a lifesaver.

If possible, before you even have your first client, have your forms ready, for whatever pleadings or other documents you will be using regularly. You'll look like a rock star when you complete the client's work more quickly than they ever expected. The bane of most lawyers is getting bogged down and not getting to the client's work on time. This often happens because of uncertainty about the next step, or anxiety about the next step, on the part of the lawyer. Forms and checklists help make it easier to get the work done quickly. Not getting the work done in a timely fashion is one of the biggest complaints of clients.

Another common client complaint is not having their calls returned, or not being kept in the loop about their case. It's easy to get so caught up in the actual work that you don't return calls, or you forget to let the client know what is developing in his case. Always copy the client on communications, to let him know you're working. Try to touch base with each client at least weekly or monthly. If the client feels that you care about him and that you are working hard for him, he will be very loyal to you, even if his case does not go well. I have found this to be almost universally true. You can have a poor outcome in a case, but if the client felt that you cared and tried hard, he won't hold it against you. On the other hand, if the client feels that you blew him off and didn't care, you can win him the moon and he will still be unhappy with you. Most clients will have no idea if you're a good lawyer or not, or if you're doing the right things or not. What they do know is how you made them feel. Treat your clients like VIPs and they will overlook your lack of experience.

Be prepared with checklists and forms, pay attention to the client, be responsive, and get the work done quickly, and you will be head and shoulders above the rest of the bar, and you will enjoy word of mouth referrals and repeat business.

PROFESSIONAL HELP

Get an accountant, if you don't want to do your own taxes. If you have formed a professional limited liability company or corporation, you may need help with your taxes, especially for the first year.

Try to find a reliable computer guru. Nothing screws up business more than not being able to use your computer, or your software. Have a phone number that you can call whenever you need help. It doesn't have to be someone local; you can use someone anywhere in the world, and they can remotely access your system and show you what to do or fix it for you. Keep in mind, though, that if you're using someone in India, when it's daytime here, it's nighttime in India, and vice versa.

CHOOSING AN AREA
OF PRACTICE

DEFINING YOUR GOALS

Which area of law is right for you? Should you try them all, taking any clients you can get? Take it from a general practitioner - it is far easier to run a boutique law firm, focusing on just one area of the law. I would recommend choosing just one area, becoming proficient in that area before deciding whether to add any others. Develop your systems and forms and get good at it. Then, if you want to take on more, you can. Don't be tempted to take whatever clients come along, just because you need the money. That is the number one mistake that many lawyers make, and it is the worst practice strategy. You will end up stressed and disorganized, and you will find that you're not doing a good job for the clients because you're having to learn a new practice area with each new case. You won't be happy, your clients won't be happy, and you will end up losing money because you have to spend so much time getting up to speed on each new matter. And your reputation will suffer. Better to stick to one area and look like you know what you're doing. (And, actually know what you're doing.)

Tip: Just because you CAN do it, doesn't mean you SHOULD do it. Learn to say "no" to clients that are not the type of business that you are looking for. Know what you want, and refer the rest to other lawyers, who will return the favor someday and refer a client to you. Try to imagine the perfect client for your chosen area, then try to market towards that client. Turn down all clients who score less than 3 or 4 on a scale of 5 in desirability (for example, a "1" is a very demanding client with a difficult case, who probably won't pay you, and a "5" is your perfect client type for your practice, easy to work with, with an easy case and willing and able to pay a handsome fee). Never, ever, take a "1" or a "2" no matter how badly you want business. You'll thank yourself later. I have never kicked myself for turning a client away but have often regretting saying yes to a case that, in retrospect, I knew was not a great case to begin with. Those cases always take way more time than you think they will, and you will lose money to boot. In the end, the client won't be happy, and neither will you. It's hard to tell people "no," especially if you like helping people, and they are sitting across the desk, looking at you so hopefully. Be prepared to tell people that you can't help them. If you're really on the fence and don't want to say no, just quote a fee so high that you hope it will deter them. Then, if they hire you anyway, maybe the case won't be a complete loser for you.

Deciding to strike out into a new area of law is a big decision. Try to pick an area that is a good fit for you. You will be investing many hours of your life into this path, so try to pick the one that is most likely to be fulfilling for you in the long run.

Here is the secret to why you will succeed: most lawyers don't do any marketing. If you actively and effectively market your practice, you will be way ahead of most practicing attorneys, and you will get business. Marketing works. And it's not hard to do. A lot of it is just making contacts. People like to send business to people they know. It takes time to build a practice, but if you have a will to succeed and are willing to get out there and work at it, you will be successful. There will come a day when you lift your head and realize that you know what you're doing, and business is rolling in effortlessly.

"No man ever achieved worth-while success who did not, at one time or other, find himself with at least one foot hanging well over the brink of failure."   *Napoleon Hill*

Don't be afraid of failing. If you have no failures, you're not trying hard enough to be all you can be; you're playing it too safe. You should not expect everything to go your way every time. Be prepared to hit some bumps, but don't give up. You will get there.

When you build your own practice, it can be whatever you want it to be. You can be a litigator, enjoying the adrenaline rush of court every week, or you can be a document nerd, quietly designing estate plans. You can build a low overhead practice that allows you to work from home and part time while spending time with your kids. Or, if you prefer, you can eventually build a big practice with a fancy office and start employing some of the other lawyers out there looking for jobs. It's up to you.

"Do one thing every day that scares you."   *Eleanor Roosevelt*

If the whole idea of building a practice feels overwhelming, just pick one area that you think you could do for extra money and start doing it. You don't have to commit to it full time. Just begin being a lawyer in some way, and it will become easier as you go along.

Here are some things to ponder as you decide which area of law to make your own.

WHAT TYPE OF PRACTICE IS IDEAL FOR YOU?

What exactly are you looking for? What makes sense for you?

__ Full time work
__ Part time or flexible work
__ Working with other lawyers
__ Working solo
__ Exciting, challenging practice vs low stress practice
__ Financial success vs helping people (The two are not necessarily mutually exclusive, but which one is your main motivation? It's okay to say financial success, if that's what's driving you – choose a practice that will be likely to meet that goal. If you're more motivated by making a difference in the lives of others, then be sure to look for a practice that will provide you with that personal satisfaction. If you want both, look for both.)

ASSESSING YOUR PERSONALITY AND STRENGTHS

C onsider your personality and your natural strengths and weaknesses.

_ Do you want to be in the courtroom?
_ Do you enjoy helping people?
_ How important is the money?
_ Are you organized?
_ Do you love legal research?
_ Do you love drafting documents?
_ Are you a detail person?
_ Do you like working with and interacting with people?
_ Are you competitive (Do you like to win?) (The corollary: can you handle losing?)
_ Do you love adrenaline?
_ Do you handle stress well?
_ Do you love the "action?" Do you enjoy telling amusing "war stories" at parties?

ASSESSING YOUR REALITIES

Consider your unique situation and circumstances.

_ Do you have any money to start a practice?

_ Can you borrow money to start a practice?

_ Will you have to practice from home, and if so, for how long?

_ Do you have a job now? If so, how much time can you carve out to practice law? Will you have to quit this job in order to build a practice? Can you work part time or flex time?

_ How much money do you need to survive?

_ How long can you wait for the payoff of profits?

_ Are you living with your parents? Can you stay there until you get a practice off the ground?

_ Do you like the area of the country in which you live? (Once you set up a practice, it's hard to move. Consider living where you want to be first, then starting the practice).

_ Do you know any other lawyers who might like to start a law firm with you?

PUBLIC SERVICE LOAN FORGIVENESS PROGRAM

Keep in mind the Public Service Loan Forgiveness Program, under which you can have your student loans forgiven after 10 years if you make 120 qualifying monthly payments while working for a qualifying employer. See http://www.nerdwallet.com/blog/loans/student-loans/student-loan-forgiveness-careers/ and http://www.equaljusticeworks.org/sites/default/files/qualifying_employment.pdf and https://studentaid.ed.gov/sa/repay-loans/forgiveness-cancellation/public-service and http://www.usnews.com/education/blogs/student-loan-ranger/2014/04/02/6-true-answers-about-public-service-student-loan-forgiveness.

The Consumer Financial Protection Bureau estimates that about one-quarter of workers in the U.S. qualify for Public Service Loan Forgiveness and fail to take advantage of it.

Make sure that, if you find yourself working for a non-profit or a governmental entity, you take advantage of the opportunity to have your student loans forgiven!

SOME AREAS OF PUBLIC SERVICE:

Administrative Law Judge
Public Defender
Attorney for Division of Child Support Enforcement
Attorney for Social Services, or the governmental department in your state that handles foster care cases

Any government organization, which includes federal, state, local, tribal organization

or college/university, or public child or family
services agency

AmeriCorps

Peace Corps

A tax-exempt nonprofit under 501(c)(3) of the IRS tax code

A nonprofit organization that provides one of following public services:

> Emergency management
> Military service
> Public safety
> Law enforcement
> Public interest law services
> Early childhood education
> Public service for individuals with disabilities
and the elderly
> Public health
> Public education
> Public library services
> School library or other school-based services

GETTING STARTED

Here's the path I recommend you follow:

Do an honest self-assessment and decide on your target practice area after reading the chapters on each area. I recommend choosing only one area. You can add more later. Some exceptions to that rule are:

> 1. If you want to do Child Custody and Support, you should also do Guardian ad Litem for the experience.
> 2. You can do Divorce and Guardian ad Litem.
> 3. You can do Child Custody and Support and Divorce together (and Guardian ad Litem as well), but it would be easier to start with Child Custody and Support first and get up to speed on that before adding Divorce.
> 4. You can do Criminal and Traffic Defense together because they are so similar.

Establish the basic requirements as described in this chapter (phone, office supplies, business cards, form a PLLC, get insurance, set up a website if recommended for your area of practice, decide where to meet with clients, etc.).

Acquire the necessary skills, forms, and procedures as set forth in the chapter on your chosen area of law and have the necessary checklists and forms ready.

Start marketing.

THE AREAS OF PRACTICE

Adoptions
Appellate Work
Bankruptcy
Child Custody and Child Support
Collections
Conservation Easements
Criminal Defense
Divorce
Elder Law
Estate Planning
Freelance Contract Lawyer
Guardian ad Litem
Guardianship and Conservatorship
Personal Injury
Real Estate Title Searcher
Social Security Disability
Traffic Defense

ADOPTIONS

OVERVIEW

The good news is, simple adoptions are relatively easy to learn and straightforward to do. The bad news is, not that many people need them, so the business is spotty. Most of the adoptions I've done as a general practitioner have been either grandparent adoptions or stepparent adoptions. Again, easy, but not so common that you can make a living doing them. Most family law attorneys do divorce, child custody and support, and adoptions. You don't have to be a family law attorney to do adoptions, though. You could simply do adoption work to supplement other income.

That said, it is a different story if you can find a niche doing adoption work for a specific agency or group (such as a private adoption agency or a governmental department doing foster care adoptions), or doing the more complicated types of adoptions, such as private placement adoptions or intercountry adoptions (which, by definition, are no longer easy, at least not in the beginning).

So, unless you can find or create your own niche, this area is mostly useful as a supplement to a more lucrative practice, such as divorce work.

WHAT IS INVOLVED?

Adoption is a statutory remedy, and each state's statutory requirements will vary somewhat. The requirements will differ for the different type of adoptions, which are, broadly:

Stepparent adoption

Close relative adoption (such as a grandparent, aunt or uncle)

Adult adoption (often a stepparent adopting the stepchild they raised, after the child turns eighteen and the absentee biological parent's consent is no longer required)

Foster care adoptions

Private placement adoptions

Private agency adoptions

Intercountry adoptions

Sometimes the process will require obtaining custody of the adoptee as a first step. Some types of adoptions require that a detailed evaluation and report be performed by the local department of social services (it may be called something else in your state). Some statutes require that the parties be counseled prior to certain adoptions.

There is a process to follow in those circumstances in which the consent of the biological parent is withheld contrary to the best interests of the child, which requires proper notice to the withholding parent, and a court hearing to determine whether the adoption should be allowed over the objection of the withholding parent. This, of course, is a fact-based finding which depends on the circumstances. Sometimes a statute will create a presumption, for instance, that the consent is being unreasonably withheld if the parent has not seen the child for 6 months or 12 months, without good reason. Another presumption may be created by your statute in the case of abuse or an "unfit" parent.

Private placement adoptions are those in which the adoptive parents wish to adopt a child of an unrelated mother and have asked you to facilitate it.

Obviously, the intercountry adoptions will be very complicated, as they require an understanding of international law, and they may need to be done first within the legal system of the country of birth, then completed in the United States.

FEES

Adoption fees will vary, depending on local standards and the requirements for that particular adoption. You can bill these with a flat rate (if you are sure you know what work will be involved), or on an hourly basis (but be sure to obtain a large retainer that you anticipate will cover the entire cost). Depending on your jurisdiction, you will generally be charging between $100 and $300 per hour. I recommend that new lawyers either charge on the lower end, because it will take you much longer to do the work at first, or charge more per hour, and do not capture all of your hours until you know what you're doing. You don't want to gain a reputation as slow and expensive.

Some clients prefer flat fees because they like to know exactly what it will cost, and hourly fees have a tendency to result in "sticker shock" when the client sees the bill. If you're billing by the hour, send the client a bill every month (or more) so that they can see how it's building up. I myself prefer flat fees because I don't have to keep track of my time, unless I just want to keep track in order to better evaluate whether my fee is appropriate for the time I spend on each case.

Basic adoptions generally generate between $2,500 and $6,000, although more complicated cases can bring in twice those figures. The most complicated adoptions, such as intercountry adoptions, can bring much higher fees, although those are generally handled through an agency, who employs an attorney to do the legal work, and sets the fee.

WHAT THE PRACTICE LOOKS LIKE

This scenario assumes you are doing basic adoptions. The scenario for private placement adoptions may include more steps, depending on the situation. The scenario for intercountry adoptions will vary greatly from what I've laid out below, as there will be many more steps involved.

1. Get a phone call from someone needing an adoption; schedule an appointment.
2. First appointment: gather information, advise client of what to expect and how long it might take, quote fee, and receive fee.
3. Open file, draft or print out the appropriate checklist for this particular type of adoption and begin drafting necessary pleadings and other documents (such as consents).
4. Schedule necessary court hearing(s).
5. Attend court hearing(s) with client.
6. Depending on your statute's requirements, follow up with further steps as necessary.
7. Make sure to order a new birth certificate.

8. Close file.
9. Receive Thank You card for display in your office.

GOOD FIT?

Adoptions are generally a low stress practice, although if you're dealing with international adoptions there may be much more pressure. An adoption is usually a feel-good case, with the adoptee and new parents happy at the end. That said, any type of practice can run into difficult, demanding clients who are going to give you grief no matter how good you are. Don't take it personally, and don't do any more work for those types, unless you charge them extra to make it worth your while.

There are court appearances to be handled, but they are usually straightforward and easy. This is a type of practice that shy, quiet, court-adverse lawyers can usually manage. You don't have to be aggressive or the captain of the debate team to succeed in adoption work.

There can be some drama involved in cases in which the biological parent objects to the adoption, and you have to prove to the court why that parent is unfit or for some other good reason should no longer be involved in the child's life. In these cases, you just study the statute and any relevant case law and make sure you have your ducks in a row and your evidence prepared. And if your case is not strong, be sure to warn your clients up front that the judge may well disagree with you (and collect your fee in advance).

You do need to have some attention to detail, as you need to be sure that you have followed all statutory requirements before you get to court. However, once you've done one, you can use that case as a blueprint for all further adoptions of that particular type. So, this is a practice that lends itself to checklists, and can eventually become very automated and easy, with an assistant eventually doing the bulk of the work.

HOW TO ACQUIRE THE SKILLS

The law is mostly statutory, meaning that you just need to find the appropriate statutory chapters on adoption for your state, and read them. Chart them. Make checklists.

Research the Continuing Legal Education offerings for your state to find seminars, books, and forms for an adoption practice.

Familiarize yourself with the court or courts that handle adoptions proceedings in your state. Meet the clerk and deputy clerks. Meet the judges. Ask questions about local practices. Although adoptions are confidential, you, as a member of the bar and an officer of the court, may be allowed to sit in on one (with consent of the judge and lawyer involved) to watch how they are done. If you do not find this opportunity, sit in on some public cases (if any) in those courts to find out where to stand and how to address the judge.

From reading the statute and from any CLE products you may find, determine what forms you will need and find, purchase, or draft them.

PRACTICE FROM HOME?

You can certainly do adoptions from your dining room table, but you will either have to meet the clients in their own homes or find a suitable place to meet with clients for each appointment. Depending on your state's statutory requirements, you may need a notary public, and perhaps a witness or two, when your client signs petitions or consents.

HOW TO BUILD THE PRACTICE

_ Website: you need a professional-looking website. See my section on websites.
_ Phone book: yes, some people still use them, so you should be in the white and yellow pages. Yellow pages ads can be expensive, so meet with a salesperson

(the meeting is free) to find out your options for placing a larger ad in the yellow pages section.

_ Talk to local lawyers who do not do adoptions. Join your local bar association and introduce yourself at their next meeting. Let the whole bar know what kind of work you're looking for.

_ Newspaper: some papers will allow you to place a free ad announcing the opening of your business, or the expansion of your business to include adoptions.

_ Networking with referral sources: Get to know the local foster care agency, and any adoption agencies near you. Let all the local churches know that you are doing adoptions – this can be a great source of referrals. Talk to some local ministers, priests, and rabbis, and see if they are willing to let you leave brochures with them, place a flyer on their bulletin board, and/or be included as an ad or an insert in their monthly newsletter.

_ Educating: Offer to speak to appropriate agencies about adoption.

_ Brochures, flyers, business cards, etc. If nothing else, you will need business cards.

_ Spread the word. Tell everyone what you're doing. Facebook. Twitter. Any way you can.

APPELLATE WORK

OVERVIEW

Establish yourself as the local guru of appeals and help other practitioners to prepare and file and/or argue their appeals. NOTE: This may be an area of work for those who are not yet licensed to practice law, if you work essentially as a contract paralegal for other lawyers and clarify that the hiring attorney is responsible for overseeing your work.

WHAT IS INVOLVED?

Appeals are governed by state law and state rules of court (unless you are in federal court, in which federal procedure and rules apply).

An appeal generally involves filing a notice within the statutory deadline, preparing the record for appeal, and identifying and briefing the issues on appeal. If the appeal is accepted by the appellate court, the next step involves arguing the appeal before a panel of appellate justices.

If your appeal is denied, you may wish to file a motion for reconsideration, if allowed under your rules.

Representing the appellee, you would monitor the appellant's notices and pleadings for compliance with law, carefully review the record to be sent to the appellate court and propose changes as necessary, review the appellant's brief and prepare a brief in response, and, if the appeal is granted, prepare and appear for oral argument.

You can certainly limit yourself to the written work of appeals, with the hiring attorney handling the oral arguments, if you wish.

FEES

Depending on the level of appeal and the issues involved, an appeal could bring anywhere from $5,000 to $50,000 in fees. In the beginning, most of your work will likely be simple appeals, and on the lower end of the fee range. You may bill hourly, or you may set a fixed fee. Until you know how much time is required, you may want to start out billing hourly.

WHAT THE PRACTICE LOOKS LIKE

1. Get a phone call from an attorney wanting help with an appeal. Discuss fee arrangement. Find out relevant dates (such as the date of the final order) to assess your deadlines.
2. Receive your fee or retainer in advance whenever possible.
3. Check the applicable deadlines and make a checklist. (Date the notice of appeal is required, deadlines for any procedures regarding preserving and preparing the record [including deadline to file transcript of proceedings, the date on which the record will be sent to the appellate court, etc.] deadline for filing brief, etc.). Refer to your local rules of court and the appellate rules of procedure.
4. Referring attorney (co-counsel or employer) gives you access to the file, which you will review and copy as necessary.
5. Visit the courthouse and review the trial court file and obtain copies of anything you don't already have. Hopefully, a court reporter was hired for the trial and there will be a transcript. If not, you will need to prepare a statement of facts in accordance with your court's rules and procedures.
6. If your referring attorney has not already done so, you will prepare a notice of appeal in accordance with local rules.
7. Prepare the record for appeal (transcript or statement of fact, plus any pleadings, discovery, and evidence which are in the court file) in accordance with local rules.

8. Prepare any other filings required by your local rules (such as questions for appeal, notice to submit transcript, etc.)
9. Research the issues, enunciate the questions for appeal, and address each question in an appellate brief.
10. Prepare and file the brief in accordance with local rules (some rules require that the brief be bound in a certain way, be of a certain type or size font, of a certain number of pages, with a cover page of a particular color or thickness of paper, etc.). Be sure to give yourself enough time to have the brief prepared by a print shop in time to mail it within the deadline.
11. If the appeal is granted, orally argue the appeal before a panel of judges.
12. If appeal is denied, file motion to reconsider, if appropriate.

GOOD FIT?

This is a relatively low stress practice, although you will need to keep on top of statutory deadlines or you will be in big trouble.

Preparing appellate briefs is a good practice for those who love to research and write.

The oral argument portion of the practice is a good fit for those who enjoy debate.

You don't have to do both; you can choose either one or offer your services in both if they both appeal to you.

HOW TO ACQUIRE THE SKILLS

Read your state appellate statutes and rules to understand the procedures for appeals in your jurisdiction. The entire procedure is statutory, so reading the appropriate chapters of the statutes and the rules of court will give you most of what you will need to know. Make a timeline of deadlines, and a checklist of what is required.

Always remember that the trial attorney cannot appeal anything that he did not object to at trial, so make sure the trial record (be it a transcript, a statement of facts, or another written record of some sort) reflects the trial attorney's objection to each issue you are appealing.

Make sure you have a good legal research system or know how to research effectively online for free. It also may be possible to use the hiring attorney's research system.

You may be able to obtain a copy of an appeal (the pleadings, motions, record of trial court proceedings, and briefs) from your appellate court, or, sometimes, from a law school library, or from a helpful attorney friend. If this is your first appeal, it would be helpful to see what the final product is supposed to look like.

Search your state's Continuing Legal Education offerings for seminars or books on appellate practice in your state.

PRACTICE FROM HOME?

This is an easy practice to manage from a home office.
You may, at times, be able to work in your hiring attorney's office.

HOW TO BUILD THE PRACTICE

_ Website. A website is not an absolute necessity if you plan to depend mostly on word of mouth referrals, but you may be able to obtain some business from one, so have one when and if you can. Sometimes lawyers are looking around for help with appeals, and you will want them to find you. Have a blog to improve your position in search results and to demonstrate that you know what you're doing Write short blogs about appellate stumbling blocks or rules – you can find fodder for these by googling around or by researching caselaw in your state for cases citing the rules or statutes governing appeals. Your blogs don't have to be long. Just show that you know a thing or two.

_ Networking with referral sources. This is the main way you will build this business. Your referral sources are other lawyers. Avoid big or medium sized firms and focus on solo practitioners or law firms with five or fewer attorneys who do not already have an appeals specialist on board. Visit lawyers in neighboring towns and rural areas and introduce yourself. Just drop in and talk to the attorney or leave your business card. Follow up in a week with a letter or email. Keep yourself "top of mind" in case they happen to need help with an appeal, by emailing or mailing them from time to time. Market routinely and systematically. If you have a blog, invite them by email to subscribe to your blog. Join your local bar association and introduce yourself at their next meeting. Let the whole bar know what kind of work you're looking for.

_ Advertise in local or statewide legal publications. This is a good way to gain exposure with other lawyers and begin to make your name recognizable as someone to call for help with appeals. The Virginia Lawyers Weekly and the monthly publication for the Virginia State Bar regularly contain ads by attorneys offering their services to other lawyers for appellate work.

BANKRUPTCY

OVERVIEW

Bankruptcy is a good option for a lawyer who wants to specialize in one area and eventually have a practice that is largely run by assistants. Bankruptcy lends itself well to systematic handling of files. It is best run as a volume business and a specialty, and not as something you do on the side, since it is important that you know what you're doing and keep up with any changes in the law in this ever-evolving field.

WHAT IS INVOLVED?

A bankruptcy lawyer helps people who are in over their head and need financial relief. The bankruptcy lawyer must know the difference between the several types of bankruptcy relief and know which one is applicable to any client's situation. The two most common types of bankruptcy relief are Chapter 7 and Chapter 13.

The bankruptcy lawyer collects financial information and documentation from the prospective client, along with an up-front fee, then processes that information through the forms and procedures that the particular client's needs require.

This practice lends itself well to heavy staffing assistance, with the staff obtaining the client's documentation, processing the information, and preparing the necessary documents, with the lawyer meeting and advising the client, reviewing the paperwork and appearing in Bankruptcy court on the client's behalf. The court appearances are usually fairly routine and rote, although the lawyer will occasionally have to deal with the demands and objections of creditors. Occasionally, a sticky question could arise which might require research and argument on the part of the lawyer.

Under Chapter 7, the client surrenders all of his non-exempt property to the Bankruptcy Trustee. The Bankruptcy Trustee will sell that property and use the proceeds to pay the creditors. At the end of the process, the client's remaining unsecured debt is "discharged," which means it's forgiven.

Clients with sufficient income will be required to file under Chapter 13. Under Chapter 13, you will work with the Bankruptcy Trustee to create a payment plan for the client's debts. The plan will last for three to five years and at the end of it, the client's remaining unsecured debt is discharged. Unlike under Chapter 7, local bankruptcy law usually sets the "presumptively reasonable" attorney fees for Chapter 13 cases. If the attorney charges the presumptively reasonable fee, the Court won't look into the charges unless specifically requested to do so.

In both Chapter 7 and Chapter 13, the lawyer's office will handle all of the administrative work. The lawyer will help the client navigate the complex rules governing Chapter 13 payment plans to create a plan that the client can handle and that will satisfy the court. If the creditors attempt to challenge the automatic stay, the plan, or the discharge, the lawyer will answer their motions and make sure that they can't take advantage of the client.

For Chapter 13 cases, the client will make regular plan payments to the Bankruptcy Trustee every month and the Trustee will pay the appropriate portion to the lawyer, and the rest to the remaining creditors as provided by the plan.

FEES

Chapter 7 clients will generally have to pay your fee up-front. Nationwide, the average attorney fee for a Chapter 7 case is $1,250. The range is generally between $750 and $2,200. The cost may vary significantly by market. You can generally expect to charge more in a large metro area than in a small town. The complexity of the case may also affect the fee. A relatively simple "no asset" case (with no non-exempt assets) will pay less than a complex case which is more likely to result in litigation.

Chapter 13 clients generally pay a certain fee up front, then the rest of the fee is collected as part of the monthly payment sent to the Bankruptcy Trustee. Nationally, the average is around $3,000, but each bankruptcy district has its own standards and rules.

WHAT THE PRACTICE LOOKS LIKE

1. Get a phone call from a person who thinks they may need to file for bankruptcy; schedule a meeting.
2. First meeting: answer the client's questions, advise them, quote and receive a fee, and hand the client over to the staff for processing. (In the beginning, you are the staff, so you will need to give the client a long list of documents and information you will need and follow up with them until you have it.)
3. Prepare the bankruptcy pleadings.
4. Second meeting with client to review bankruptcy pleadings.
5. File the pleadings with the appropriate bankruptcy court.
6. Appear in bankruptcy court for necessary hearing(s).
7. Respond to any motions filed by creditors.
8. Follow up as required until the case is closed.

GOOD FIT?

This is generally a lower stress practice, although your clients may be highly stressed and need a lot of hand holding (preferably by your staff).

The court hearings are usually not very adversarial. Often, the whole process is done on paper, with the court appearance being quite routine; essentially a rubber-stamping of the paperwork. Sometimes, however, some argument is required to respond to the concerns, objections, or demands of a creditor, or to respond to the bankruptcy judge if he or she has questions or concerns about your client's situation.

HOW TO ACQUIRE THE SKILLS

Bankruptcy is a statutory remedy, and, as such, all you really need to do is to know the law. This is not be as easy as it sounds, however. Bankruptcy is governed by both federal law and state law, and you will need to know how the two intersect.

It is ultimately a challenging and complex field. However, it can be a very successful niche practice, and one well worth pursuing. Here's how to get started.

Read about Bankruptcy basics in the publication of the Administrative Office of the U.S. Courts on the website below. It provides basic information to the general public on different aspects of federal bankruptcy laws, and answers some of the most commonly asked questions.

http://www.uscourts.gov/services-forms/bankruptcy/bankruptcy-basics

Join the American Bankruptcy Institute: http://www.abi.org/membership. This organization will connect you to a community of bankruptcy professionals, offers continuing legal education, news and resources. Sign up for their Bankruptcy 101 course, which reviews bankruptcy fundamentals for new practitioners: http://www.abi.org/education-events/bankruptcy-101.

For further resources, join the National Association of Consumer Bankruptcy Attorneys: http://www.nacba.org/membership/member-benefits/.

(If you are still a law student, find out if your school offers bankruptcy internships or clinics.)

PRACTICE FROM HOME?

You can practice bankruptcy law from home, but you will need somewhere to meet your clients, unless you are willing to meet with them in their homes. Certain paperwork may require a notary public and/or witnesses.

HOW TO BUILD THE PRACTICE

– Marketing to lawyers: Most lawyers do not do bankruptcy, because it is a dangerous thing to do if you haven't brought yourself up to speed in this technical area of practice. Many lawyers do, however, have clients that need bankruptcy advice and assistance. Therefore, many lawyers will need someone to refer their clients to for bankruptcy issues. Take your business cards door to door and introduce yourself to as many lawyers as you can, especially general practitioners, family law attorneys, real estate lawyers, personal injury lawyers, social security disability lawyers, and criminal defense attorneys. If they don't already know a bankruptcy attorney whom they respect and send clients to, they may well send you some work.

_ Website. A good website is a necessity. See my chapter on Websites.

_ Phone book. Yes, you should be in the phone book, especially under "Bankruptcy" in the yellow pages. Make sure your ad is at least as good as the other bankruptcy lawyers in the book, if you can afford it.

_ Newspaper: a regular ad is a good idea. If nothing else, take out an announcement ad when you open your business (often this will be a fee ad).

_ Networking with referral sources: other lawyers are your best referral sources. Court them. Other referral sources might include churches, clubs, and service organizations. Also consider realtors, who may know sellers in financial distress. Join your local bar association and introduce yourself at their next meeting. Let the whole bar know what kind of work you're looking for.

_ Educating: Never turn down an opportunity to talk to groups about bankruptcy. In fact, seek out these opportunities. Start with groups that you belong to, or who already know you.

_ Brochures, business cards, etc. You must have business cards, and it's a good idea to have a brochure or flyer to leave in appropriate spaces.

_ Spread the word. Tell everyone you know what you're doing. Ask them to spread the word. Facebook. Twitter. Do whatever you can to get the word out.

_ Billboards. If you find a reasonably-priced billboard, consider renting it.

_ Local radio. Local radio stations can be a great way to get your name out there. Take out an ad, or offer to be interviewed on a talk show.

CHILD CUSTODY AND CHILD SUPPORT

OVERVIEW

Child custody and child support cases are plentiful and common. They are often the "bread and butter" of general practitioners and family law attorneys. Once you have done a few, they become fairly routine, especially child support, which is mostly just doing the math.

WHAT IS INVOLVED?

Child custody: represent a parent, grandparent, or other party who is pursuing custody and/or visitation of a child or children.

Child support: represent a parent, grandparent, or other party who is seeking to obtain, increase, decrease, or discontinue child support.

Child custody cases are similar to divorce cases in that they can be highly emotional and dramatic, and you often don't know that you are representing the bad guy in the situation until you are too far into it to get out. Client hand holding is necessary, as is strict client control (control of client's expectations, and control and guidance of client's goals). You will often have to be stern with your clients and tell them things they don't want to hear, like "you have to tell your stripper girlfriend to move out," or "it's not possible to keep the father from ever seeing the kids again, that's just unreasonable."

Read my chapter on Divorce to get a feel for the emotional content of these cases. Pure child custody, without divorce, however, can often be quicker and easier, as in many states it is pursued in lower court or even a special family court, rather than the more formal court in which divorce cases are (in some states) required to be filed. Different discovery rules can apply in lower court or family court, as well. It varies from state to state, but that is how it is in Virginia. In some states, the family court hears both divorces and custody cases. Check your state's court system and jurisdictional rules (found in the state statute and rules of court, but often also on the court's website).

Child support cases can be quick, routine, and financially rewarding, especially in volume. It is possible to develop a reputation for just being the best child support attorney around, although most often, lawyers who do child support also do custody, as they often go hand in hand. For instance, if you file for a change in child support and the other side counters with a petition to change custody, you will have to address both custody and child support at the hearing.

One factor to understand in child support matters is your state's Division of Child Support Enforcement (CSE or DCSE), which collects child support payments and allocates them to the custodian(s) of the child or children of the payor. In some states, the custodial parent may apply for child support directly with the CSE office, while in other states the court will transfer the file to CSE once initial child support has been established. In Virginia, it is optional, and the court will ask the parties whether they want the payments to go through CSE. Sometimes, the court is tired of seeing the same parties over and over again and orders the case to CSE over the parties' objections.

When CSE is involved, a lawyer for the custodial parent (parent with custody, or the payee) becomes optional, because the CSE lawyer is advocating for reasonable child support. However, either party can still employ a private lawyer, and the payor parent should certainly do so.

FEES

The average fee for a child custody case is between $1,500 and $5,000, depending on where you live and your local standards. Fees for child custody cases can range from $500 to a very quick and simple matter, such as an uncontested change of custody, all the way up to $40,000 for high end litigation involving many depositions and expert witnesses.

You can charge a flat fee, or, more commonly, ask for a large retainer and then charge hourly against the retainer, sending a bill for more if you run through the retainer. Hourly rates vary but are usually between $100 and $400 per hour. Many attorneys charge a higher rate for time spent in court, with a lower rate for all other work.

The fee charged for a child support case is entirely dependent on the circumstances, especially how much the lawyer may be able to save the payor spouse, or how much the payee spouse may be able to get. Many times these are quoted as a flat fixed fee, although they can also be done hourly. Be sure to get your retainer up front whenever possible – you don't have time to be collecting fees from your clients after the case is over (when they are no longer highly motivated to pay).

WHAT THE PRACTICE LOOKS LIKE

1. Get a phone call from an unhappy parent looking for help in a child custody situation. They may be "fee shopping" and only want to know your fee. Convince them to schedule a free appointment, or, quote a fee and schedule an appointment.
2. Meet with client to gather as much factual information as possible, and to receive your fee or retainer. (Keep in mind that everything your potential client tells you may or may not be true or provable in court, so expect surprises and charge accordingly).
3. Note as counsel with the court if there are pending proceedings (and note the court date on your calendar) or prepare to draft the appropriate petition.
4. Obtain copies of all previous court orders and pleadings.
5. Draft petition if necessary. This may be just a fill-in-the-blanks court form. (Note: some jurisdictions require the petitioner to go through a court intake officer in order to file in family court; check your state's rules and/or ask the clerk's office about local procedure.)
6. Talk to the child or children, if appropriate. Do a home visit if appropriate or ask your client to bring in pictures of their home.
7. If a guardian ad litem is appointed to represent the children, advise your client how to meet with and talk to the GAL.
8. Do whatever discovery you may deem necessary, if allowed in your court.
9. Attempt to negotiate a settlement with opposing counsel or opposing party, if appropriate
10. Subpoena witnesses (family, friends, school teachers, doctors, counselors, etc.)

11. Request a subpoena duces tecum for any documents you may wish to introduce, such as school records, medical records, counseling records, or employment/financial records for child support calculations.
12. Meet with and prepare witnesses and client for court hearing.
13. Attend court hearing.
14. Explain the outcome to the client.
15. The judge may ask you to prepare the final order, or your court may use its own forms.
16. Discuss appeal options with the client, if applicable.
17. Send client a closing letter with a copy of the court order.

GOOD FIT?

Child custody and child support practice is fast paced, and the custody cases can be quite stressful. The support cases are not as stressful, but the two usually go hand in hand.

Child custody is not for the tender-hearted, as the battles can be vicious. Also, you may find yourself on the wrong side of a battle and have to advocate for a position you find distasteful. Nothing is uglier than what people do to each other in family court. That said, though, it is a great way to make a living, as there is no shortage of business.

You will be in court all the time, and quickly develop your courtroom skills, which can be a great education and great experience if you want to transition into other litigation work, although you won't be doing any jury trials, and your experience will be in family court. Still, you will get a feel for the rules of evidence and common evidentiary objections and basic courtroom etiquette. It would be easy to transition to criminal defense, for instance, and gain your jury trial experience once you get there.

If you do a good job in the courtroom, the local foster care agency may notice, and you could land a job working for your state's foster care program. The beauty of this track is that you may be eligible for the Public Service Loan Forgiveness Program, under which you can have your student loans forgiven after 10 years if you make 120 qualifying monthly payments while working for a qualifying employer. See my chapter on Public Service Loan Forgiveness for more information.

Handling child support cases is a good way to set yourself up to apply as an experienced applicant for regular employment with the state's Division of Child Support Enforcement, if you're looking for a steady state job. This track may also make you eligible for the Public Service Loan Forgiveness Program. See my chapter on Public Service Loan Forgiveness for more information.

HOW TO ACQUIRE THE SKILLS

Being a guardian ad litem for children is an excellent way to learn the necessary skills to represent parents in custody and visitation cases. As a guardian ad litem in the courtroom, you will see many lawyers representing parents, and watch many doing it right, and many doing it ineffectively. You will see what works with the judges and what doesn't. It's a safe and easy way to get invaluable trial experience, and get paid doing it. And if people like what they see, you will soon be getting calls from parents asking you to represent them. See my chapter on Guardian ad Litem.

If you don't want to start out as a guardian ad litem, that's okay. You can learn this practice much the same way you would learn to do criminal practice: by watching court whenever possible. Family court is generally not open to the public, but, as a lawyer, you will usually be permitted to sit in any time. Just introduce yourself to the judge and ask for permission to watch court. The judge may require the parties to consent to your presence, or not, depending on the judge and the sensitivity of the case. Judges are typically happy to let new lawyers sit in the courtroom to watch.

Find your state's statutes concerning child custody, support, and visitation, and read everything. It's a good idea to have a basic understanding of abuse and neglect proceedings as well as foster care, because sometimes those issues will come up.

Read the rules and procedures for your state's family court, including procedures for appealing a ruling to a higher court.

Look for Continuing Legal Education offerings (seminars and publications) in your state regarding child custody and support. They might be included in a broader publication or seminar on family law or divorce law.

If your state or your Continuing Education providers publish an evidence handbook, I'd advise getting one for anyone interested in doing litigation. Virginia has an excellent one, and it even comes in digital format. Keep this with you in court for those times when you are just stumped and don't know the evidentiary rule at hand. You will also refer to it often when preparing for trial.

PRACTICE FROM HOME?

You can start doing this practice from home, but you will need a place to meet with clients and witnesses. You can start out by meeting your client at the courthouse (or the jail) if you need to, but as soon as you can swing it, get your own office. You'll be able to charge higher fees with a straight face.

HOW TO BUILD THE PRACTICE

_ Website: a website is a good idea, as people use the internet more and more to find lawyers. Make sure that your website makes you look like THE custody and support lawyer to turn to. Having a blog helps your search ratings and helps to capture people who are googling around trying to figure out how to represent themselves in family court.

_ Phone book: you should be in the white pages, and the yellow pages is also a good idea, as it will most likely capture you some business if you advertise that you focus on child custody and support. The yellow pages are not cheap, though, so you might start with a small ad your first year, and expand later if you can afford it.

_ Referral sources: Other lawyers who don't handle child custody and support are the best referral sources. It is also good to let area churches and synagogues know you can help their folks with custody or support issues. Let them know you will talk to their folks at no charge, and answer their questions (if, in fact, you choose to offer free initial consultations, which you may want to do at first, to get your business off the ground.) Join your local bar association and introduce yourself at their next meeting. Let the whole bar know what kind of work you're looking for.

_ Educating: talking to groups gets your name out there as an expert in child custody and support. Offer to talk to groups and offer to write articles for newspapers or other publications on something like "10 ways to improve your chances of winning your custody case" or "5 ways that grandparents can obtain court-ordered visitation rights." Mention that you give fee initial consultations (if you do).

_ Spread the word. Tell everyone you know. Facebook. Twitter. Join and volunteer as much as you, to meet more people and let them know that child support and custody cases are what you do.

COLLECTIONS

OVERVIEW

Collections is the process of collecting the money owed by a debtor to a creditor. Your client will be the creditor, usually a business. The debtor owes the business money. You take legal means to collect it.

WHAT IS INVOLVED?

- Writing collection letters to debtors
- Filing suit (usually in lower court or small claims court) against the debtor
- Appearing in court to obtain a judgment against the debtor
- Pursuing further avenues to collect the debt
- Debtor's interrogatories;
- Execution against the debtor's bank accounts or personal property;
- Garnishment of the debtor's wages;
- Docketing the judgment as a lien against any real estate the debtor may own; and/or
- Filing a lawsuit to sell the debtor's real estate to satisfy the debt.

This is the type of practice that works best as a specialty, in which you do nothing but collections (or very little else). It works best in volume, since you can get a system going, utilize staff to do most of the paperwork (basically everything except appearing in court), and run everything through the system.

I have found that it is not advantageous to do a few collections here and there, although, if you are just starting out and need the work to build your business, it might be better than nothing. Doing a few collections takes almost as much work as doing a lot of collections, and the fee per case is low. You may have to sit in court all morning waiting for your cases, which is okay if you have fifteen or twenty cases, but a real waste of time if you only have one or two. Collections is best done as a high volume, low fee per case business. Another reason that I prefer collections as a boutique practice is that you are going to gain a reputation as that scary mean lawyer who sues people and garnishes their pay. If you're simultaneously trying to establish an elder law practice as a kind helpful lawyer, for instance, the cognitive dissonance might lose you some customers. Either you're the nice guy, or you're the mean guy. Choose one and own it. I suppose you could be creative and be a nice guy collections attorney, but in my experience, fear is the main motivator that gets most of these folks to pay their judgments. They are afraid of losing their big screen TV or their home and they are afraid of having their wages garnished, and if they think you'll be patient with them, they will walk all over you. Debtors, in my experience, will lie, lie, lie. If you're a softie, either choose another field, or be prepared to become jaded.

FEES

Your fee is usually a percentage of the money collected, often 25% to 40%. The client also pays the court costs and related expenses.

WHAT THE PRACTICE LOOKS LIKE

1. Get a debt from your creditor client, or several debts on their books.
2. Begin your collections process, first by yourself, and later, hopefully, with your assistant doing most of the work.
3. Write collection letters to debtors
4. File suit (usually in lower court or small claims court) against the debtor
5. Appear in court to obtain a judgment against the debtor
6. Pursue further avenues to collect the debt
7. Debtor's interrogatories;
8. Execution against the debtor's bank accounts or personal property;

9. Garnishment of the debtor's wages;
10. Docketing the judgment as a lien against any real estate the debtor may own; and/or
11. Filing a lawsuit to sell the debtor's real estate to satisfy the debt.

The most common collection technique is garnishment of wages, but tracking down deadbeats who keep changing jobs can make it difficult. I have had great success with executions against their personal property, and also with docketing judgments when the debtor owns real estate.

GOOD FIT?

This is not a "feel good" practice, although you and your client will feel good if you can collect the debts and get you both paid.

If you feel sorry for a person when you hear about how his child is sick and his wife lost her job and his ailing parents live with them and he hurt his back and they are about to lose their house and their car died and they just had to put their dog to sleep, this is probably not the practice for you. You will often be trying to squeeze money out of people who have very little, and often have very sad stories to back up their failures. As much as you will feel sorry for folks, if your client doesn't get paid, neither do you.

This is a relatively low stress practice. The court appearances are rote and routine, and generally pretty tame. Quite often, the debtor does not even show up. They rarely show up with their own lawyer.

HOW TO ACQUIRE THE SKILLS

Become acquainted with your local court procedures for judgments and debt collections. This is not rocket science. Debt collection is pretty cut-and-dried. Read the statutes relating to small claims and lawsuits. Find out which court handles small debts (the jurisdictional limit is usually under $20,000 or so, and very often the limit is as low as $5,000, or even $2,000). Go to that court's website and read all information there and peruse any forms the court may provide. Often, the lower court will have a form that can be filled in to collect a debt. Visit the courthouse, get to know the clerk and assistant clerks, and ask them for forms and brochures regarding their procedures.

Find out when that court is in session and what days the court handles debt claims (the clerks can tell you this, or the court website may list this information). Go to court and sit in the back row and just watch what happens. This is a good way to learn your local procedures: where to stand, how to address the judge, how debt claims are generally handled in your area. See what happens when the debtor shows up, and when he doesn't.

When you're ready to get started, introduce yourself to the judge and let him or her know that you intend to be practicing in his or her court doing collections.

Research the continuing legal education opportunities in your state to find seminars or state-specific materials on collection practices.

Collect or draft the following forms:

_ Letter to the debtor stating that you represent the creditor, and requesting payment (copy the creditor).
_ Debt warrant or other standard form petition that your lower court and/or other court uses to obtain a judgment against a debtor.

> _ Make a checklist of all requirements for
> this form.

_ Garnishment forms for your local court.

> _ Make a checklist of all requirements for
> this form.

Find out your local procedure to docket a judgment as a lien against real estate. In Virginia, we go to the lower court (General District Court) and ask for a transcript of the judgment. Then we take it across the hall to the upper court that deals with real estate (Circuit Court), where the real estate deed records are kept, and tell the clerk there that we want to docket the judgment. They know what to do. In Virginia and most other states, docketing the judgment where the deed records are kept makes the judgment a lien against any real estate in the debtor's name. If the debtor tries to sell or mortgage any real estate with a lien against it, he will be required to pay off the lien.

Find out your local procedures for executing against a debtor's bank accounts or real property and collect or draft any forms you many need to use, together with checklists of requirements.

At some point in your practice, you may need to learn how to file a lawsuit requesting the court (upper court or Circuit Court in Virginia) to sell real estate to collect a debt.

PRACTICE FROM HOME?

You can easily be a collections attorney from your dining room table. You can meet your creditor clients at their place of business, and draft all of your necessary paperwork from your home office. If you need to meet with any debtors, you can meet them at the courthouse.

HOW TO BUILD THE PRACTICE

_ Website
_ Phone book
_ Networking with business owners and other creditors will be your best marketing strategy. Go to any and all local businesses (especially the smaller ones), ask if they could use help collecting their unpaid debts, and beat your competitor's prices, if necessary. Many business owners do their own collections. For these folks, you will have to sell them on the time savings you can provide, for they will be able to just hand their debts over to you and forget them. When you collect, they will get a check. The business owner or bookkeeper has to prepare the legal documents, appear in court and often sit all morning waiting for their cases to be heard, and then prepare the garnishments. They usually are not familiar with other methods of debt collection, although they might know enough to docket a lien, and the savvier ones will be able to look up the debtor's real estate holdings, if any. They certainly would not be able to petition the court to sell the debtor's real estate without legal assistance. Getting the judgment is

just the first step and does not get them paid. Executing on the judgment gets them paid.
- You will need business cards. It couldn't hurt to design and print a brochure discussing your services. You can use the same language and images that you use for your website.
- Spread the word. Tell your friends, your church, your clubs and other organizations what you do. Join a church, join the rotary, the Kiwanis, etc., to develop business relationships that can lead to business. Volunteer to sit on the boards of charities. Be active in your community. Community activity will bring you in contact with business owners, and that can lead to business, because most businesses need to collect debts.
- Join your local bar association and introduce yourself at their next meeting. Let the whole bar know what kind of work you're looking for. Lots of the local lawyers won't want to handle collections and may be happy to refer cases to you.

- There are many out-of-town debt-collection companies that contact our firm asking us to appear on their behalf (so they don't have to drive to our jurisdiction). for $100 per case, more or less (they often schedule more than one case in court on any given day). It's all negotiable, so the fee is not set in stone. These firms found us, and not the other way around, but do some searching for collection firms and companies in large cities in your state that are more than an hour's drive from you and contact them to let them know you are willing to appear on their behalf in your jurisdiction.

CONSERVATION EASEMENTS

OVERVIEW

A conservation easement is an easement (a right attaching to a parcel of land) that has some type of conservation as its purpose. A conservation easement is given by the landowner to the easement holder. The easement holder is either a governmental entity or a private land conservation organization (usually a "land trust").

A landowner has the right to use his land in any way he wishes, as long as the use is not prohibited by land use ordinances or other laws. A conservation easement places controls on the future use of that land, for conservation purposes.

The conservation purposes are many, such as to preserve historically important sites, to preserve and maintain forests, to protect watersheds, to prevent or limit development of open lands, preservation of wildlife corridors, or any number of purposes or combination of purposes as are appropriate to the land and to the easement holder's goals and objectives. Each easement is crafted individually and negotiated to achieve both the easement holder's objectives and the landowner's objectives.

The conservation easement is perpetual, or permanent. The deed of easement is recorded in the local land records and becomes part of the chain of title for that parcel of land. The landowner still owns the land, and can use, sell, or pass the land down to future generations in any way he sees fit, as long as his use of the land does not violate the terms of the conservation easement. The easement holder has the right to monitor the use of the land in order to ensure compliance with and enforce the terms of the easement.

WHAT IS INVOLVED?

The reason that conservation easements can be a source of income for lawyers is that there are valuable tax advantages to donating a conservation easement. People need help with these easements, and, while they are a worthwhile endeavor in and of themselves, they also can generate valuable tax deductions, and, in some states, real cash money.

One of the most important incentives is the federal conservation tax deduction, which allows landowners to deduct all or part of the value of a donated easement from their taxable income. The conservation tax incentive which was ratified in 2015:

- Raises the deduction a donor can take for donating a conservation easement from 30 percent of his or her income in any year to 50 percent;
- Allows qualifying farmers and ranchers to deduct up to 100 percent of their income; and
- Extends the carry-forward period for a donor to take tax deductions for a voluntary conservation agreement from 5 to 15 years.

These changes apply to donations made at any time in 2015 and to all donations made after that. This is a powerful tool for allowing modest-income donors to receive greater credit for donating a very valuable conservation easement on property they own.

State Income Tax Credits for Conservation

o In addition to the federal tax deduction, 16 states offer some form of tax credit for conservation easement donations. Many state incentives apply to fee-simple donation of land as well as conservation easements.
o The most powerful state tax incentives for conservation are the transferable tax credits available in Colorado, Georgia, New Mexico, South Carolina and Virginia. In these states, if a landowner donates an easement but doesn't owe enough tax to use the full credit, he or she can sell the remaining credit to another taxpayer, generating immediate income.
o Nine states offer some form of non-transferable income tax credit — Arkansas, California, Connecticut, Delaware, Iowa, Maryland, Massachusetts, Mississippi and New York. The New York tax credit is unique, offered not at the time of donation, but every year in an amount equivalent to 25% of the property taxes paid on land under easement.

o   In Virginia, we have the transferable state tax credits for conservation easements, and this can be a real boon for farmers or others wishing to conserve or preserve their land, especially if they are looking for cash to make improvements to the farm (or for any other purpose). For instance, a client of ours had a large farm, which he never wanted to see broken up or developed. We helped him to place a conservation easement on the land, accomplishing his goals, and in exchange, he received huge federal tax deductions, in addition to more than $100,000 worth of Virginia tax credits, which he immediately sold at 80 to 90 cents on the dollar, generating more than $80,000 in cash just for doing something he would happily have done for free. Our fee was $10,000.

FEES

According to some sources, the legal fees range from $10,000 to $40,000 in states which offer valuable tax credits that can be converted to cash. The greater the value of the land, the greater the potential cash. In states that only offer the federal tax credits, the attorneys' fees are likely to be much lower.

WHAT THE PRACTICE LOOKS LIKE

1. Get a phone call from a landowner considering a conservation easement. Schedule an appointment.
2. Meet with the client, get information about his land and what kind of easement he may be considering. Discuss his options. Quote a fee. (The fee may be received up front or you may receive a retainer up front and the remainder of the fee after the easement is donated and the tax credits earned.) Sign a retainer agreement.
3. Gather the necessary information about the land (the deed, the tax assessment, and any prior appraisals).

4. Contact one or more land trusts or governmental organizations to begin discussing an easement. They will send you their information and easement forms.
5. Order an appraisal by someone familiar with conservation easements – you will want the land appraised before and after the easement to document the reduction in value as a result of the easement. (The appraisal to be paid for by the client).
6. Work with the land trust or governmental organization to draft an easement that will meet your client's needs. (The land trust or other easement holder will usually send you a draft of their preferred easement as a starting point.) Get your client's approval.
7. Execute the agreed-upon easement and be sure that it is recorded in the deed books at the appropriate clerk's office.
8. Walk your client through the steps necessary to take advantage of the federal tax deductions and state tax credits, including converting the state tax credits to cash.
9. Collect the remainder of your fee.

GOOD FIT?

This is a pleasant, low stress practice, with a green feel.

The best states for conservation easement work on those which provide the most powerful tax credits: Colorado, Georgia, New Mexico, South Carolina and Virginia. If you plan to practice in one of these states, conservation easement work can definitely be worthwhile.

If you are not in one of these states, your fees will be much lower and the work somewhat harder to come by.

Conservation easements are low stress and rewarding work, and, once you've done one or two, they are not very hard to master. Attention to detail is a plus. Documents nerd will especially enjoy this work, although it is not nearly as challenging or as detail oriented as estate planning or elder law Medicaid planning. The easements are already drafted but may need to be tweaked.

It helps to have some knowledge of real estate law, or at least a working knowledge of real estate titles, deeds, and easements. See my chapter on Real Estate.

HOW TO ACQUIRE THE SKILLS

Googling around will tell you most of what you need to know about conservation easements. Visit The Land Trust Alliance website. http://www.landtrustalliance.org/what-you-can-do/conserve-your-land/benefits-landowners. They have a wealth of information about conservation easements.

See also the Nature Conservancy's site www.nature.org.

Search for land trusts and governmental organizations accepting conservation easements in your state. Get their information and copies of their easement forms. Make a list of the various organizations and the types of conservation easements they offer.

If you are in a tax credit state, Google around and/or talk to the land trust/governmental organizations in your area to find out where and how to sell tax credits in your state. Get any necessary forms and familiarize yourself with them.

Talk to a local accountant about how to use federal tax credits for conservation easements. If you like his or her answer, refer your clients to the accountant for tax advice.

Bone up on real estate essentials. See my chapter on Real Estate.

PRACTICE FROM HOME?

This practice lends itself well to a home office, if you are willing to meet the clients at their homes or on their land.

HOW TO BUILD THE PRACTICE

_ Website: a good website and a blog are highly recommended.
_ Phone book and yellow pages if you can afford them.
_ Newspaper: place at least an initial announcement, and place small regular ads touting the benefits of conservation easements if it is affordable in your area.

_ Referral sources: other lawyers who do not handle conservation easements are good sources of client referrals. Join your local bar association and introduce yourself at their next meeting. Let the whole bar know what kind of work you're looking for. Real estate agents may also be a source of referrals, as well as accountants and financial advisors, especially if you take the time to educate them on the financial benefits of donating a conservation easement. Get in touch with your local Farm Bureau Insurance agent and let them know how you can help their farmer clients, who are prime candidates for conservation easements.

_ Educating: Giving talks about the benefits of conservation easements is a great way to market your practice. Talk to organic farmers, farmers in general, land owners, conservation groups, accountants and financial advisors, etc. Be prepared for people to ask a lot of questions about loss of control of their land. They don't understand easements, and it scares them. You need to put them at ease.

_ Brochures, business cards, etc. Place flyers at health food stores, farmers markets, tractor supply stores, feed stores, and any other venues likely to draw green, ecologically minded people, and/or farmers.

_ Direct mail: If allowed in your state, go to the courthouse and, using the tax map and landowner information, identify lands which are prime for conservation easements and send a letter and/or brochure to targeted landowners about the potential benefits of donating a conservation easement, stressing that you offer free consultations.

_ Spread the word. Tell everyone you know what you do. Twitter and Facebook. Join groups and clubs and churches. Volunteer and socialize.

CRIMINAL DEFENSE

OVERVIEW

You will represent clients charged with criminal offenses, from minor misdemeanors to serious felonies. This is not to suggest that you have to take every type of case that presents itself, however. Most criminal defense attorneys rarely handle murder cases and will consider co-counseling or simply referring the case to someone who routinely handles such charges. White collar crime is another subspecialty that most criminal defense lawyers would not feel comfortable undertaking without assistance. It is therefore possible to specialize in certain types of crimes such as white-collar crime, manslaughter/murder, or sexual offenses, and charge much higher fees for such charges.

The criminal defense lawyer almost always handles traffic offenses as well. You should read the chapter on traffic defense in conjunction with this section.

Although it is also possible specialize in defending federal criminal offenses, I will not address that niche in this chapter. Much of what I have written, however, will apply to a federal practice as well, if you substitute the word "federal" for "state." I am not familiar enough with the federal criminal defense practice to write intelligently about how to build such a practice.

WHAT IS INVOLVED?

You will advise clients charged with criminal offenses, letting them know what kind of fines or jail time to expect. Often, your clients are in jail and will need to be bonded out, and you will handle the bond hearing. You will need to acquire a feeling for your local judges and know what they are likely to do in any given situation. You will work frequently with the local prosecutors to try to obtain favorable plea bargains, where the client pleads guilty or "no contest" in exchange for a guaranteed outcome or sentence, whether that is having the charges dismissed after a certain period of good behavior, being convicted without jail time, or going to jail for a guaranteed length of time rather than risk the maximum sentence in court. Those cases that cannot be "pled out" will go to trial, and you will handle the bench trial or jury trial. You will also advise the unsuccessful client regarding his appeal options, and either handle the appeal, or engage a co-counsel to assist with the appeal. You may also try to get your client creative sentencing alternatives, such as work release or attending a substance abuse program.

FEES

The fees can be quite substantial, and a busy criminal defense practice can be a lucrative business. Minor misdemeanors may bring a few hundred dollars, while felonies will bring thousands in fees. The fee for a misdemeanor is generally somewhere between $500 and $3,000. Felonies are generally charged at between $5,000 and $10,000, although the fee can be $25,000 or more for very serious charges or especially problematic cases.

The fees will be substantially higher in all categories for those cases that need to be taken to a jury trial. (This is a decision which is made on a case-by-case basis, by determining based on the lawyer's experience whether a plea bargain, bench trial, or jury trial is the best route for a particular situation).

Some cases will end up taking more time than you expected, while others will unexpectedly end in a plea bargain, so some cases will be more lucrative than others. Most criminal defense lawyers charge a flat rate fee, rather than by the hour. If you do charge by the hour, your fee can be anywhere between $100 to $400 per hour, and even more after you are very experienced and have a great reputation.

WHAT THE PRACTICE LOOKS LIKE

1. Get a phone call from a new client charged with a crime. Get all pertinent information, answer the usual questions, and give the usual advise about not

talking to anyone, etc. Quote a fee and let the client know that you will not note as counsel with the court, or begin to represent them, until you receive the fee in full.

2. Receive the fee in full. Note as counsel with the court (write a letter to the court advising that you are representing the client in that matter). Note the hearing date and any other deadlines on your calendar.
3. Meet with the client and all witnesses to get as many facts as possible.
4. File a motion for discovery, if appropriate.
5. Review the court file and any evidence the prosecutor is required to share with you under your state's discovery rules.
6. Evaluate the case for the necessity of any pretrial motions, such as a motion to suppress the evidence.
7. Talk to the prosecutor to determine if a favorable plea agreement can be achieved.
8. File any pretrial motions, brief them if necessary, and argue them to the judge at a hearing.
9. Subpoena witnesses (family, friends, school teachers, doctors, counselors, etc.)
10. Prepare your client and witnesses for trial. Have your evidence ready.
11. Try the case.
12. Your court may require a separate sentencing hearing, if your client is convicted.
13. Explain the outcome to the client.
14. If convicted, note the deadline for appeal and discuss appeal options with the client. Follow up with a dispositional letter which outlines the outcome and also discusses appellate rights.
15. Handle any sentencing issues. Your client may want to serve his jail time on weekends with work release, or in another jurisdiction, etc.
16. Appeal if necessary. (Obtain appeal fee first).

GOOD FIT?

If you'd rather talk and argue than research and write, and you're not keen on minute details, you'll like this practice. Especially if you are good at thinking on your feet and coming up with creative arguments or responses. If you enjoy negotiation, even better. If you like a good fight, like to win, and get off on adrenaline, this one's definitely for you.

The simple misdemeanor cases are not very stressful, but with the more serious charges, your client will have a lot on the line, including jail or prison, and therefore it places more responsibility on your shoulders and creates a much higher stress level for you as well. If your client is convicted, he may well lose his spouse, lose custody of his children, lose his job, and lose his car, his home, and all of his money, as well as his reputation. Be sure that you are ready to stand next to this client and hear the sentence and be ready to feel that impact with him and explain it to him. In my experience, though, if you've fought hard for him, he will not hold it against you, and he will appreciate that you cared enough to give it your all. Oftentimes, the criminal client is not accustomed to having anyone in his life back him up and fight for him, and he will be very appreciative, even if he is convicted. He will blame it on the judge or jury. If, however, he feels that you were just interested in your fee and didn't care about him, he certainly will blame the conviction on you.

Showing that you care about your criminal defense clients, and putting up a good and aggressive fight, will earn you a good reputation at the jail, where the convicts are all talking about their lawyers. Soon, you will have business coming in from word of mouth. Repeat offenders are good business, as long as they can keep coming up with the fees.

Developing experience as a criminal defense attorney can put you in a good position to apply for a job as an assistant prosecutor, arguably one of the best jobs a lawyer can get (low stress, good pay, good benefits).

Your experience can also can put you in a good position to apply for a job as a public defender, which pays less and can be very high stress, but it will put you on track for having your student loans forgiven after ten years under the Public Service Loan Forgiveness Program. See my chapter on Public Service Loan Forgiveness Program.

HOW TO ACQUIRE THE SKILLS

Each criminal charge is statutory, and so the statute that defines the offense will tell you exactly what the prosecutor will need to prove in order to convict. Your job is to know exactly what the prosecutor needs to prove, and look for defenses, weaknesses, deficiencies, or loopholes.

Technology provides defenses. The results of lab tests must be introduced properly into evidence, sometimes requiring the lab technician to appear at trial.

Constitutional challenges provide loopholes, particularly with regard to the "stop," the "search" and the "seizure." You must learn all you can about when the police can legally stop a person or a vehicle. If they didn't have the right to stop them in the first place, your client can skate. Learn all you can about when the police can search a person, backpack, bag, vehicle, home, or building. If the search was illegal, the fruits of the search are inadmissible in evidence. Learn all you can about what a "seizure" is – how long the police can detain someone, and when that becomes illegal.

Sometimes, your client is just plain guilty, and you will be trying to obtain the best plea agreement you can get from the prosecutor.

Look for Continuing Legal Education offerings (seminars and publications) in your state regarding criminal defense. Try to find one that offers forms for discovery and motions. Read up on criminal procedure. Look also for publications or seminars on defending serious traffic offenses.

Read your state's entire chapter on criminal offenses. Know the different levels of misdemeanors and felonies, and how much jail time each can bring. Read the entire chapter on criminal procedure.

Sit in on your local court's criminal docket and watch what happens at both the lower court level and the upper court, including jury trials. (Call the clerk's office or go online to find out what days each court hears criminal matters). Watch how evidence is introduced, and what objections are most commonly raised. Get to know your prosecutors and your judges. Get a feel for how it works, and for what a good plea bargain might look like. Find out what your judge is likely to do with someone who hit his girlfriend and was charged with assault and battery. Get a feel for what a normal outcome is on a possession of marijuana or crack cocaine, and what the normal outcome is for a second charge. See how bond hearings work, and how probation violation hearings work. Spend a lot of time watching court, until you start to feel like you can guess what the outcome of most common charges will be. Then you will be ready.

If your state publishes a Judge's Deskbook, buy one or try to get your hands on one. (See if the local bar has a law library and look to see what books it contains). In Virginia, there is a Judge's Deskbook for Circuit Court (upper court), and a Judge's Deskbook for General District Court (lower court). These are invaluable. They are designed to be an easy reference for judges to use when they are unsure of the law. For instance, what are the exceptions to the hearsay rule? When can a police officer stop someone who is just walking down the street? Those kinds of answers are at your fingertips in these deskbooks.

If your state or your Continuing Education providers publish an evidence handbook, I'd advise getting one for anyone interested in doing litigation. Virginia has an excellent one, and it even comes in digital format. Keep this with you in court for those times when you are just stumped and don't know the evidentiary rule at hand. You will also refer to it often when preparing for trial.

In Virginia, there is a two-volume set of criminal jury instructions that have been approved by the courts. You can buy them. I'm sure it's similar in your state. As long as you are using the approved instructions, you are golden. Actually, it's a great practice to look at the jury instructions first, early in the case, because they will tell you exactly what you will need to prove.

One great way to quickly become experienced in criminal defense is to get on your jurisdiction's Court Appointed Lawyer list. In some areas, you will be swamped with work in no time, while in other areas, where there is a full-time public defender, you might not get as much work. Court Appointed criminal defense work typically does not pay very well, although that varies greatly from state to state. Even in Virginia, where the pay is relatively low, you can still make a fair living if you do enough of it. The beauty of it is that you can do it for a year or two to jump start your criminal defense practice, then stop taking court appointed work and enjoy the private fees that you will earn from the many referrals that come your way due to your work as an aggressive and respected court appointed lawyer.

PRACTICE FROM HOME?

You can start doing this practice from home, but you will need a place to meet with clients and witnesses. You can start out by meeting your client at the courthouse (or the jail) if you need to, but as soon as you can swing it, get your own office. You'll be able to charge higher fees with a straight face.

HOW TO BUILD THE PRACTICE

_ Website: a website is a good idea, as people use the internet more and more to find lawyers. Make sure that your website makes you look like THE criminal lawyer to turn to. Having a blog helps your search ratings and helps to capture people who are googling around trying to figure out how to defend themselves.

- Phone book: you should be in the white pages, and the yellow pages is also a good idea, as it will most likely capture you some business if you advertise that you focus on criminal defense. The yellow pages are not cheap, though, so you might start with a small ad your first year, and expand later if you can afford it.
- Referral sources: Other lawyers who don't do criminal law are the best referral sources, especially general practitioners and family lawyers. Join your local bar association and introduce yourself at their next meeting. Let the whole bar know what kind of work you're looking for. It is also good to let area churches and synagogues know you are doing criminal defense, in case a minister, priest or rabbi has a parishioner in trouble. Let them know you will talk to the alleged perp at no charge and answer their questions. Join your local bar association and introduce yourself at their next meeting. Let the whole bar know what kind of work you're looking for.
- Educating: talking to groups gets your name out there as an expert in criminal defense. Offer to talk to groups (including high school and college students) and offer to write articles for newspapers or other publications on what to do if you're stopped by the police, or what your rights may be if charged with a crime. Mention that you give fee initial consultations.
- If possible in your jurisdiction, get on the Court Appointed Lawyer list. Do this work for a year or two to jump start your criminal defense practice, then stop taking court appointed work when your private practice is humming.
- Direct mailing. In Virginia, we see a lot of direct mailing, and it appears to work, especially in traffic cases. Some lawyers routinely check the court's docket (or the docket of several courts in a geographical area) to get the names and addresses of people with new charges. They then send a form letter and business card to these folks, touting themselves as the best defense lawyer to call. Check with your state bar to be sure that it's allowed in your state, and also be sure that the language of the letter complies with your state's ethical standards for advertising by lawyers. There are companies, such as http://www.arrestrecordmarketing.com who, for a fee per letter, will send letters out on your letterhead to all people charged under your chosen criminal statutes in your jurisdiction. These letters often produce clients.
- Spread the word. Tell everyone you know. Facebook. Twitter. Join and volunteer as much as you, to meet more people and let them know that criminal cases are your specialty.
- This website offers a ton of ideas on how to set up and market a criminal defense practice:
  http://criminaldefense.homestead.com/lawofficemanagement.html#anchor_32

DIVORCE

OVERVIEW

Divorce law can be a lucrative business. Divorce is common, and it's expensive. Develop a reputation as a good divorce lawyer, and you will never lack for business.

WHAT IS INVOLVED?

The good news: you can make a great living helping people through divorces.

The bad news: you have to help people through divorces. People in divorce are a special kind of crazy, no matter how sane they were before the divorce began. Everybody responds differently to a divorce situation, but it is an extremely stressful, emotional time for all, and it tends to bring out the worst in many. The divorce practice involves a lot of emotional phone calls from clients, sometimes at all hours of the day or night, and a lot of hand holding. If you don't like getting calls at 2am on Sunday and don't have time for daily hand holding, you will have to learn to be very stern with your clients, and set firm rules about what they can expect, and what you will or will not allow.

One ugly fact about divorce practice is that you don't really get to choose your clients. I mean, you do, but you won't know if you're on the ugly side of a case until it's too late. Every new client who comes in to hire you will shed a tear as they tell you a tale of woe so compelling that makes you think the other spouse is a sociopath at best, and perhaps the actual spawn of Satan. Then, after you take the case and get halfway through it and can no longer back out, you find out that the actual spawn of Satan is your client, and that you really can't stand the son of a bitch, and don't like the nasty things he wants you to do to his soon-to-be ex-wife. This is where you will hone your persuasive people skills trying to convince him not to use the children as pawns in a vicious tug of war, et cetera. Eventually, you will be able to spot these types more effectively and quote twice your normal fee hoping they will go elsewhere.

That said, divorce is an area that lends itself well to automation and structure, and eventually you can have your staff do most of the grunt work and hand holding. The best way to practice divorce law is to do nothing but divorce, or nothing but family law, and have a well-structured system, with forms and checklists, so that each case is handled in an efficient and effective manner, with much staff involvement. Once you have a staff-run office, your main roles will be client control, giving legal advice, reviewing pleadings, discovery, and agreements, and attending hearings. (At the hearings, don't be surprised if your vicious cross-examination reduces a witness to tears. These can be very emotional and dramatic cases).

Many lawyers do divorces as part of a general practice, and that's fine, too, but if you're doing a few divorces here and there along with other work, you will quickly find that the divorces are your least favorite cases and you wish you weren't doing them. If you plan to do divorce as part of a general practice anyway, try to take the time to create a structured system with forms and checklists, and involve staff as much as possible, to prevent burnout.

FEES

Most divorces are billed hourly (average $100 to $400 per hour), although sometimes you can try a flat fee, for example if the case will be uncontested. (Warning: a large percentage of new divorce clients will tell you that the case will be uncontested. Only a small percentage of them will actually end up being uncontested).

Statistics say that the average attorney fee for a divorce is between $15,000 and $30,000.

Depending on the case, each divorce can bring anywhere from $1,500 for a truly uncontested divorce that only needs paperwork (some lawyers will do it for as little as $500), to $5,000 for a minor contested case with few assets, and on up to $40,000 to $100,000 or more for handling the divorce of a doctor or wealthy client who has significant assets to fight over, especially where alimony and/or child support may be involved. Sadly, the most vicious divorces produce the highest attorneys' fees.

WHAT THE PRACTICE LOOKS LIKE

1. Get a phone call from a new client; set an appointment.
2. Gather information, quote fee, collect the largest retainer you can.
3. Open file, begin running the case through the necessary checklist and procedure. For a divorce, you will generally prepare a lawsuit for divorce or, if one has already been filed, prepare a response to it.
4. Ask for a guardian ad litem to represent the children in appropriate cases. Advise client to meet with the GAL and prepare client for that meeting.
5. File a motion for pendente lite relief – asking the court for a temporary order to establish the status quo while the case is in litigation. This is a very important hearing, as the order will often cover child custody and support, temporary alimony, and possession of the marital home. This will often set the tone for the final divorce decree.
6. Conduct discovery to ascertain the extent and nature of the couples' assets.
7. Attempt to achieve an amicable settlement.
8. Go to trial if necessary.
9. Draft final order of divorce and any other documents necessary to effectuate the division of property.

GOOD FIT?

Divorce law is not for the faint-hearted. It requires a certain strength of character to handle the clients. It is a high stress practice, as your clients will be under high stress, can often be very demanding, and often placing high expectations on your performance. In high asset cases, there is a lot on the line, and your pressure and responsibility will be high.

If you're willing to take on the demands of the practice, however, you will eventually have your office running like a fine machine and have your client control skills well honed. Then it will be easier.

Litigation is mandatory. You must be willing to duke it out in court in often ugly battles, amidst sordid lies, steamy reveals, tears, high stakes, and much drama. If you like that kind of thing, this may be the practice for you.

HOW TO ACQUIRE THE SKILLS

For only $149.95, you can purchase The Complete Guide to Divorce Practice: Forms and Procedures for the Lawyer, Fourth Edition from the American Bar Association:
http://shop.americanbar.org/eBus/Store/ProductDetails.aspx?productId=214483. This is a great way to get you started.

Keep in mind that your state's requirements will vary. Look around for a similar manual or system with forms for your particular state. Be sure that it is current, or at least recently written or updated, since laws tend to change. Go to your state's code and search for all new laws or amendments after the date of its publication.

If possible, sit in on divorce hearings in your jurisdiction. Get to know how the other lawyers handle themselves, and what to expect from your judges. This will be well worth your time.

PRACTICE FROM HOME?

This is a tough practice to handle from home, although you could certainly start out that way if you need to.

Look for an available witness room or library in the courthouse where you can meet with clients until you get your own office.

If you absolutely have no other option, you can meet with them in their own homes. Yes, they will find that somewhat odd. But a lawyer's gotta do what a lawyer's gotta do until she can find another way. Meeting in a coffee shop or restaurant is not a good option because of confidentiality issues.

HOW TO BUILD THE PRACTICE

_ Website: you will need one. See my chapter on Websites.

_ Phone book: you need to be in it, both in the white and the yellow pages, if you can swing it.

_ Newspaper: place a regular ad if you can afford it, but if nothing else, try to place an announcement of your new practice, especially if your paper offers it as a free service.

_ Networking with referral sources: Other lawyers who don't do divorces are great referral sources, especially those who do general practice (excluding divorce), who probably turn away more potential divorce clients than you can shake a stick at. Talk to small firms and solo practitioners who do real estate, criminal defense, estate planning, bankruptcy, etc., and let them know that you are available for divorce referrals. Join your local bar association and introduce yourself at their next meeting. Let the whole bar know what kind of work you're looking for.

_ Educating: you may offer to give talks to groups such as churches and clubs, regarding divorce-related or family law-related issues (adoption, custody, support, alimony, separation agreements, prenuptial agreements).

_ Spread the word. Tell everyone you know that you're doing divorces. Everyone knows someone who's getting a divorce or will be soon.

ELDER LAW

OVERVIEW

Elder law is a growing field of law, and one with much potential for success.

An elder law practice can include estate planning (wills, powers of attorney, and trusts), probate, guardian ad litem practice (representing incompetent adults), and guardianships/conservatorships, as well as the more technical and specialized area of Medicaid planning.

I cover estate planning, guardian ad litem, and guardianships elsewhere, so I am going to focus here on the more specialized and technical area of elder law, Medicaid planning.

WHAT IS INVOLVED?

Medicaid planning is a very specialized practice, and not many lawyers know how to do it. It's also not that easy to learn. But don't lose hope, I'll tell you what to do. The good news is, because it is so specialized, your competition for business will be less than you would find in more common areas of practice. You can also co-counsel with, or get referrals from, non-elder law lawyers who have clients needing this type of work (especially estate planners, general practitioners, and real estate attorneys).

Just mention the word "Medicaid" to most lawyers and they will begin to fidget and their eyes will glaze over. Most lawyers don't know much about Medicaid, nor do they wish to learn. That's why it's a good field to be in. Not many people do it.

What is Medicaid Planning?

Medicaid planning is helping people protect their assets when they need long term care (nursing home care). Without such help, a single person who needs nursing home care will be required to spend down all of their life savings, sell their home and spend that down, too, on nursing home care or other allowed expenditures (such as a prepaid burial plan), until they have less than $2,000 in assets remaining. Then, Medicaid will pay the nursing home bill. The rules are different for a married applicant – Medicaid will look at the assets owned by both spouses combined, then require that at least half of that be spent down before being eligible for Medicaid.

Medicaid planning involves pre-planning and "crisis" planning. Pre-planning means planning ahead by moving assets into a specially designed irrevocable trust that will protect those assets after the lookback period of five years has passed. If the client does not have five years, but needs long term care now, that is crisis planning, and requires an intimate understanding of the Medicaid regulations, but a knowledgeable Medicaid planner can usually save about half of a single person's assets, and often all, or nearly all, of a married applicant's assets.

FEES

A Medicaid planning case will generally bring a fee of $2,500 for a pre-planning case (for a client who does not yet need Medicaid but wants to protect assets), to $10,000 or more for a Medicaid crisis case (where the client needs nursing home care and wants to protect assets and qualify for Medicaid immediately). This is a "feel-good" practice, because you will be helping people to protect their homes and life savings from the cost of nursing home care by getting them qualified for Medicaid without losing everything.

WHAT THE PRACTICE LOOKS LIKE

1. Get a phone call from a potential client; answer a lot of the usual questions; schedule meeting.
2. Initial meeting with client: gather information about their situation. Tell them how much money you can save them and quote a fee for preparing a Medicaid

plan specific to their situation. Receive the fee in full and schedule a follow-up meeting.

3. Prepare the Medicaid plan. The plan may include such work as preparing a Medicaid application (with documentation received from the client), drafting an irrevocable trust, drafting wills, powers of attorney, drafting promissory notes, and obtaining annuities or life insurance products for the client.

4. Second meeting with client to review plan. Quote fee for implementation of plan. (Note: some lawyers quote one flat fee for preparing and implementing the plan, while others charge one fee for the plan, and a separate fee for the implementation. Once you have a little experience with it, you will find what works best for you.)

5. Draft documents in accordance with plan.

6. Third meeting with client: execute the documents and implement plan as necessary.

7. Follow-up meeting(s) or phone calls as necessary.

When you first start out, you may have to do all of the grunt work yourself to save money, but as soon as you can afford an assistant, it will make the trust funding and the Medicaid application process much less time consuming, especially the client management part (obtaining necessary documents from the client, which can require a lot of nagging and repeat phone calls).

A mature elder law practice will make good use of assistants and paralegals, freeing the lawyer up to do mostly the planning and trust drafting.

GOOD FIT?

This is a good fit for "document nerds" and people who like to do research and pay attention to details. It is not such a good fit for those of you with short attention spans who hate to read boring regulations and can't be bothered to do math or make sure that all the T's are crossed and the I's dotted. It also helps if you like old people, because many of your clients will be in their eighties and nineties. Often, you will be dealing with their middle-aged children, though, as power of attorney for Mom or Dad.

HOW TO ACQUIRE THE SKILLS

Several years ago, I decided that I wanted to be an elder law attorney, and I transitioned my practice to mostly elder law over the period of a year or two. I will tell you how I did it. You can accomplish the transition faster than I did, since I was busy with an existing practice when I began, whereas, presumably, you are not. But I did have the advantage of being able to draw clients from our existing practice, whereas you will have to do marketing to get your practice off the ground. But, it's not hard, and I'll tell you what to do.

(Insider tip: If you have an office, it should be on the first floor, and if possible, have a first-floor bathroom. Also, avoid upholstered furniture in your elder law office, conference room, or waiting room. Many older folks refuse to wear adult diapers, even though they really should).

I recommend that if you want to take on this very technical field, you should join an organization such as Eldercounsel (http://www.eldercounsel.com). They will provide you with the expertise and even the forms that you will need to practice in this field. It will still be a steep learning curve, but you will have a field of experts at Eldercounsel to turn to for assistance. You should find out when their next Elder Law Immersion & Practice-Building Camp will be held, sign up for Eldercounsel and register for the camp, a three day intensive seminar which will teach you the basics of elder law and even give you marketing tips. As a member of Eldercounsel, you will be able to use their amazing document production software which includes all the forms you will need as an elder law attorney. Eldercounsel provides a lot of educational materials for their members at no extra cost. You will also have access to several list-serves on which you can post questions to other Eldercounsel members and also monitor the questions and answers posted by others. You can even search the archives to find answers to your questions.

Elder counsel is not cheap. There is a significant down payment required (I believe a couple of thousand dollars), as well as several hundred dollars per month to be a member, and you have to sign up for at least a year. The camp is an additional cost of about $1,000 or more, plus airfare and hotel accommodations. So, you will need to invest several thousand up front, plus be able to pay a few hundred a month for a year, to get started. However, it will kick-start your elder law career and it will be well worth it. To acquire the same level of knowledge and expertise, not to mention document forms, on your own, would be extremely difficult and ill-advised, and you would not have the ongoing support provided by the Eldercounsel community. Don't try to do this type of practice on without thw support of a group like Eldercounsel. You could get yourself into hot water quickly. And your first Medicaid crisis case with a fee of $10,000 will recoup your entire initial investment.

PRACTICE FROM HOME?

You can be an elder law attorney from your dining room table, but you will either have to meet the clients in their own homes or nursing home or find a suitable place to meet with clients for each appointment (which will likely take one to two hours). You will also need a notary public, and sometimes a witness or two, to execute wills, trusts, and powers of attorney.

Your best bet would be to arrange to occasionally use space in the office of an attorney who does not do elder law, but may be able to co-counsel with you or refer clients to you, such as a general practitioner (a great source of referrals or co-counseling opportunities) or an estate planner (many estate planners do not do Medicaid planning, although many of their clients need it). Real estate attorneys also often have clients who, unbeknownst to them, need Medicaid planning. When grandma's health begins to fail, she will often ask an attorney for a deed of gift so she can give her real estate to a child or grandchild, thinking that this is a good way to protect it in the event she should need nursing home care. This is usually not a good idea for her, and this is the moment that she needs the advice of an elder law attorney.

A lawyer who has a totally unrelated practice, such as criminal defense or bankruptcy, may be happy to "rent" office space to you on an as-needed basis, and also provide access to their notary public.

HOW TO BUILD THE PRACTICE

In my experience, there are a lot of folks out there who need Medicaid planning and don't even know it exists. Once you start talking to people, you will be surprised how many people either need your help or know someone who needs your help. It's just a matter of finding those in need and letting them know how you can help.

Referral sources are an important way to ensure that clients continue to come in by word of mouth. Just one good referral source can send you a client every month. Cultivate several sources, and you will be well on your way to financial success.

Many lawyers are completely unaware of Medicaid planning and the fact that their existing clients might need it. Reach out to your local bar and let them know how you can help their clients, and even co-counsel for a share of the fee.

_ Website.. You should have a well-designed website, with a blog. This does not have to be difficult, or expensive. See section on Websites.
_ Phone book. Who uses the yellow pages anymore? Old people, that's who. I get a lot of elder law business from my yellow pages ad.
_ Newspaper. If you can afford it, place a newspaper ad. I found that the cheapest way to do this was in the "Services" section of the paper, where I could buy a 1.5 inch square ad for $10/week. Newspaper ads are probably more likely to be read in small towns and rural areas, where the entire paper is small enough to be read front to back.
_ Other lawyers. Other lawyers who don't do estate planning need to know who you are so that they can refer clients to you. Begin to build relationships with them through local bar meetings and events, and even by stopping by to introduce yourself. If you spot a lawyer that you are particularly interested in working with, invite them to lunch. Join your local bar association and introduce yourself at their next meeting. Let the whole bar know what kind of work you're looking for.
_ Networking with referral sources. It is vitally important to develop referral contacts for your elder law practice. You should meet and court the following types:
_ Hospital discharge personnel (the ones who send folks to a nursing home)
_ Administrators and business office managers of nursing homes, assisted living facilities, and retirement communities
_ Agencies responsible for maintaining senior centers and the like
_ Folks at the local Medicaid office
_ Realtors (grandma has to sell her house when she goes to the nursing home)
_ Funeral directors (grandma needs a prepaid burial plan when she goes to the nursing home)
_ Financial planners and accountants (they know when grandma enters the nursing home)
_ Educating. This may be the best way to get your name out there and make contacts at the same time. Give talks at churches, nursing homes, libraries, assisted living facilities, etc. regarding the importance of Medicaid planning, the importance of a power of attorney, or whatever they want to hear about. Talk anywhere they will let you.

_ Even better, plan an event titled "Getting your ducks in a row" or "Senior law day" etc. Find sponsors to donate space, lunches, drinks. Ask local financial planners, nursing home administrators, etc. to speak about what folks need to know to be prepared for advanced age. For instance, ask someone to speak about long-term care insurance (they will be thrilled that you are providing this marketing opportunity for them), someone else to talk about reverse mortgages, someone (perhaps a nursing home administrator or business manager) to talk about the different kind of Medicare coverage, and which ones are best, maybe ask someone from an Alzheimer's support group to talk about Alzheimer's, and you can talk about wills, powers of attorney, and Medicaid planning.

_ Brochures, business cards, etc. You will need to have these to hand out at educational and networking events. You may also be able to leave brochures at the waiting room of nursing homes, funeral directors, and the like.

_ Spread the word. Start with people you know. Facebook. Twitter. Your church, your friends. Tell everyone you know what you are doing, and you will be surprised how quickly you will find someone who needs your help. In time, it will snowball and you will have word-of-mouth referrals. Don't give up. Lots of people need this kind of legal help. The trick is to find them or help them find you. Most people don't even know that this kind of help exists, and neither do their lawyers. Get out there and talk to everyone you can and let them know what you can do.

ESTATE PLANNING

OVERVIEW

An estate planning practice involves the design of lifetime and after-death plans for people, usually through the drafting of wills, powers of attorney, and trusts. The practice can also involve the management of trust assets as a trustee.

Although an estate planner often also does guardianship and sometimes elder law, I cover those topics under separate chapters. An estate planner also often gets involved in probate, which, although an excellent area of practice and one I would recommend, will not be covered in this book due to time constraints.

WHAT IS INVOLVED?

For this discussion, I will not include estate planning for taxable estates (at the time of this writing, a single person must have over five million in assets to have a taxable estate, and for a married couple, over ten million). To do that kind of work, you will need to know both general estate planning and advanced tax planning, which is beyond the scope of this outline. If you choose to do estate planning and find yourself presented with a client who has a taxable estate, simply co-counsel with another lawyer who does taxable estates. Don't try to do it yourself.

Who needs estate planning? Lots of folks. Everyone should have at least a will, power of attorney, and advance medical directive. Beyond that, the use of revocable living trusts for asset control and protection from creditors, as well as probate avoidance, can be beneficial to anyone with savings or real estate. For instance, farmers are in special need of estate planning, as their wealth is largely tied up in the farm, rather than liquid assets, and they often need assistance protecting that asset and handing it down to one or more children who are working the farm, while providing some inheritance for their other children.

One nice thing about an estate planning practice is that it is clean. You are retained by a client, you design the estate plan, you draft the documents, have them executed, and fund the trusts. Then, you're done. Close the file. These matters don't normally drag on and on. You open a file, do the work, close the file. Move on.

FEES

Estate planning fees can range from $500 for a simple will, power of attorney, to many thousands for a complicated estate plan involving taxable estates. A typical estate plan for a non-taxable estate (under five million) involving one or more revocable living trusts would probably be billed at $1,500 to $6,500, depending on complexity.

WHAT THE PRACTICE LOOKS LIKE

Estate planning

1. Get a phone call from a potential client; answer a lot of the usual questions; schedule meeting.
2. Initial meeting with client: gather information. Discuss their needs, come up with a plan, and quote a fee. Receive the fee (either in full, or half up front and half upon execution of the documents) and schedule a follow-up meeting.
3. Prepare the documents. The plan will usually include one or more revocable trusts, will, power of attorney, and advance medical directive. You will also need to assist the client in funding their trust (moving assets into the trust).
4. Second meeting with client to execute documents and fund trust.
5. Follow-up meeting(s) or phone calls as necessary until all documents are executed and trust is funded.

Trust management

If acting as trustee for a client's trust, simply do whatever is required when asked to do so, and make sure the appropriate tax documents are filed each year. The trust should state the appropriate fee, usually a percentage of the trust assets.

Other

You may occasionally be asked to revise an existing estate plan, or perform trust administration, to remove assets from a trust or change the trust in some way.

Once your practice is up and running, a good assistant can help with many of your tasks, such as trust funding.

GOOD FIT?

This is a good fit for "document nerds" and people who like to do research and pay attention to details. It is not such a good fit for those of you with short attention spans who don't like details and would rather be engaged in lively debate. It is generally a fairly low stress practice, and your time can be easily managed, since there are few deadlines and generally no court appearances. It's a good option for those requiring a flexible work schedule.

HOW TO ACQUIRE THE SKILLS

The best way to get up to speed in a short period of time is to join an organization such as Wealthcounsel (https://www.wealthcounsel.com). They will provide you with the expertise and even the forms that you will need to practice in this field. There will be an initial learning curve, but you will have a field of experts at Wealthcounsel to turn to for assistance. You should find out when their next

Estate Planning Essentials course will be held, sign up for Wealthcounsel and register for the course, a two day intensive seminar which will teach you the basics of estate planning. As a member of Wealthcounsel, you will be able to use their amazing document production software which includes all the forms you will need as an estate planning attorney. Wealthcounsel provides a lot of educational materials for their members at no extra cost. You will also have access to several list-serves on which you can post questions to other Wealthcounsel members and also monitor the questions and answers posted by others. You can even search the archives to find answers to your questions. And, for an additional cost, Wealthcounsel can provide private mentoring or coaching, as well as practice development assistance.

Wealthcounsel is not cheap. There is a significant down payment required (I believe a couple of thousand dollars), as well as several hundred dollars per month to be a member, and you have to sign up for at least a year. The camp is an additional cost of about $1,000 or more, plus airfare and hotel accommodations. So, you will need to invest several thousand up front, plus be able to pay a few hundred a month for a year, to get started. However, it will teach you estate planning and kick-start your estate planning career and it will be well worth it. To acquire the same level of knowledge and expertise, not to mention document forms, on your own, would be time consuming and difficult, and you would not have the ongoing support provided by the Wealthcounsel community.

Your first two estate planning cases, each with a fee of $4,500 will recoup your entire initial Wealthcounsel investment.

To start a practice without joining Wealthcounsel (or a similar organization), I would recommend researching the Continuing Legal Education offerings for your state, to find one on the basics of Estate Planning. Search also for estate planning forms for your state that you may be able to download or purchase. Read all you can about how to draft, fund, and use revocable living trusts. Learn the basics of wills in your state and get a basic will form, as well as a basic revocable living trust form, a general durable power of attorney, and an advance medical directive and living will.

Learn the basics of probate (because your clients will die and their children will come to you for guidance).

Learn the basics of guardianship/conservatorship because you need to at least know what tht is and generally how it works. See my chapter on Guardianship/Conservatorship.

PRACTICE FROM HOME?

You can be an estate planning attorney from your dining room table, but you will either have to meet the clients in their own homes or residential facility or find a suitable place to meet with clients for each appointment (which will likely take one to two hours). You will also need a notary public, and sometimes a witness or two, to execute wills, trusts, and powers of attorney.

Your best bet would be to arrange to occasionally use space in the office of an attorney who does not do estate planning but may be able to co-counsel with you or refer clients to you, such as a general practitioner (a great source of referrals or co-counseling opportunities) or a real estate attorney.

A lawyer who has a totally unrelated practice, such as criminal defense or bankruptcy, may be happy to "rent" office space to you on an as-needed basis, and also provide access to their notary public.

HOW TO BUILD THE PRACTICE

There are a lot of folks out there who need estate planning and either don't even know it or keep putting it off.

_ Other lawyers. Other lawyers who don't do estate planning need to know who you are so that they can refer clients to you. Begin to build relationships with them through local bar meetings and events, and even by stopping by their offices to introduce yourself. If you spot a lawyer that you are particularly interested in working with, invite him or her to lunch. Join your local bar association and introduce yourself at their next meeting. Let the whole bar know what kind of work you're looking for.
_ Website. You should have a well-designed website, with a blog. This does not have to be difficult, or expensive. See section on Websites.
_ Phone book. You should consider being listed in the phone book, because older people still use it.
_ Networking with referral sources. Develop referral contacts for your estate planning practice. You should meet and court accountants, financial planners, insurance agents, and anyone else selling financial products to folks.

- Educating. This may be the best way to get your name out there and make contacts at the same time. Give talks at churches, nursing homes, libraries, assisted living facilities, etc. regarding the importance of estate planning, the importance of a power of attorney, or whatever they want to hear about. Talk anywhere they will let you.
- Brochures, business cards, etc. You will need to have these to hand out at educational and networking events. You may also be able to leave brochures at the waiting room of accountants, financial planners, and the like.
- Spread the word. Start with people you know. Facebook. Twitter. Your church, your friends. Tell everyone you know what you are doing.
- Be a joiner. Join a church, join the rotary club, join the country club, volunteer to serve on the board of a local charity. The more people who know you and know what you do, the more business you will get sent your way.
- Don't give up. Every contact you make adds up, and at some point, you will reach critical mass and have a successful practice.
- When you meet people, be positive. Even if you have no confidence in yourself at this point, fake it. Nobody's going to send clients to you out of pity. They have to believe that you will do a good job, or at least genuinely care about them and try to do a good job. Remember that you are marketing yourself. This is sales. Present your product in a good light. With enough practice, you will eventually be as good as you are saying (or should be saying) that you are.

FREELANCE CONTRACT LAWYER

OVERVIEW

A freelance, or "contract" lawyer, as I am referring to it here, is a lawyer who works freelance for other lawyers as an independent contractor, usually on an as-needed and temporary basis. NOTE: This may be an area of work for those who are not yet licensed to practice law, if you work essentially as a contract paralegal for other lawyers and clarify that the hiring attorney is responsible for overseeing your work.

When I was a young lawyer, terrified, and with next to no experience and no desire to go anywhere near a courtroom, I offered my services to other lawyers in my community as a contract lawyer. The only skill I had at the time besides legal research was that I knew how to search a real estate title. I was in a small town in Virginia, and there were few title companies doing their own title searches there at the time, so I found several lawyers who had been doing their own title searches and agreed to hire me on a trial basis. Once they got to know me, they asked me to do legal research. Then, one of them asked me to work on his personal injury files (which always seemed to be on the back burner), and he taught me everything he knew about personal injury. Then, other solo lawyers wanted me to help them with their personal injury cases, and they taught me what they knew. In a few years, I knew more than anyone else around about how to handle personal injury cases. That led to a full-time position with a successful lawyer who did criminal defense, personal injury and real estate work. Years later, I became a partner with a different lawyer and, although we had a general practice, we were very successful in pursuing the occasional personal injury and medical malpractice cases, enjoying some settlements in the six and seven figure range.

My work as a contract lawyer started out slowly, but as word spread of the convenience of my services and the quality of my work, I was offered more and more work, until I had to continually raise my hourly rate just to control the in-flow.

WHAT IS INVOLVED?

The freelance contract lawyer works for other lawyers on an as-needed, temporary basis, doing whatever work is required. Depending on the hiring lawyer's practice, that could be legal research, real estate title searches, drafting pleadings, motions, or discovery, drafting responses to discovery, document review, or even appearing in court to obtain a judgment against a debtor. I was often asked to assist with appeals, preparing the notices, the record on appeal, and the brief. The possibilities are endless.

Sometimes the hiring attorney will hand you a file, tell you what it's about generally, and admit that he/she has no idea what to do with it. You figure it out.

Sometimes they will want you to work on a particular type of case, like personal injury files, and help move them from beginning to end, perhaps even sitting as co-counsel at trial.

FEES

Your hourly rate will be completely dependent on what the market will bear. If no one knows you and they seem leery, and you're just starting out, give them a rate they can't refuse. Then, if they like you, give you more work and recommend you to others, you can raise your rates over time until you find what your market will bear.

For certain tasks, such as a brief court appearance, you can charge a flat rate.

WHAT THE PRACTICE LOOKS LIKE

1. Get a phone call from a lawyer needing your help.
2. Do the required work (research, draft documents, discovery, etc.)
3. Submit the work, submit a bill.
4. Get paid.

GOOD FIT?

This is an excellent way for a new lawyer with few skills to start out, gaining experience and vital contacts along the way. It is also a very low stress career path, and in addition allows great flexibility and little overhead.

It works especially well in small cities or rural areas, where lawyers have little access to experienced paralegals and are often hard-pressed to find quality assistance. It can work just as well in an urban area, however. The trick is to find the right lawyers to work for and convince them to give you a try.

HOW TO ACQUIRE THE SKILLS

The only thing you really ought to know is how to do legal research, which they taught you in law school. The rest, you will learn on the job.

Make sure you have a good legal research system or know how to research effectively online for free. It also may be possible to use the hiring attorney's research system.

The beauty of this practice is, your hiring attorney will train you. They probably didn't hire you expecting to train you, but if you are stuck or have a question, you ask them. They are usually happy to share their knowledge and expertise with you. Don't be afraid to ask. Even seasoned lawyers don't know the answers to a surprising number of questions – you will get used to that. Only if you practice in one area for a very long time do you ever get to the point where you don't have many questions any more. It's expected that you will have questions, especially if you're new. Your hiring lawyer may not know the answer, either, and you may sometimes just have to keep digging on your own until you find it.

As a young lawyer, it was a real eye-opener to learn how little the experienced lawyers around me really knew, and that even the judges have lots of questions and areas about which they know very little. I had assumed that everyone else around me knew the answers when, in reality, no one knows all of them. Don't be afraid to admit to your hiring attorney that you have questions. In fact, if you don't have any questions at all, he may start to suspect that you're faking it, and may even wonder if he can trust your work. Asking questions actually raises your trustworthiness.

PRACTICE FROM HOME?

This type of practice is almost always a home-based practice, although your hiring attorney may give you a space in their office to work.

HOW TO BUILD THE PRACTICE

You should obtain your own E&O (malpractice) insurance coverage, since you are an independent contractor and generally not covered by the hiring lawyers' policies.

_ Website: this is one of the few areas of practice for which you don't really need a website.
_ A business card is nice to have, but not essential.
_ Spread the word. Door to door marketing will be required to get your proverbial foot in the door. Visit law offices, introduce yourself, let them know your rates and abilities, and leave your business card. If you don't hear back from them, follow up with a phone call and/or letter. Don't give up until someone hires you. Once you get started, the ball will start rolling. Join your local bar association and introduce yourself at their next meeting. Let the whole bar know that you're available for contract work.
_ A busy solo practitioner, in need of occasional or temporary assistance, but not willing to commit to hiring an employee, is the perfect client for the freelance contract lawyer. Once this lawyer hires you for a job, if you do a good job, he or she will likely hire you again and again and tell his or her colleagues about you.

GUARDIAN AD LITEM

OVERVIEW

A Guardian ad Litem is a lawyer appointed by a court to represent the interests of a person under a disability, such as a minor or an incompetent adult. The appointment is for the limited duration of a pending court proceeding.

WHAT IS INVOLVED?

When a person involved in a legal action cannot adequately represent his or her own interests, the court may appoint a guardian ad litem to protect the person's interests.

Broadly, there are two types of guardians ad litem: those representing children, and those representing incapacitated (or allegedly incapacitated) adults.

Unlike typical guardians or conservators, guardians ad litem only protect their wards' interests in a single suit or legal action. Courts most frequently appoint guardians ad litem for children in parents' disputes over child custody and visitation. A guardian ad litem is also routinely appointed for a child in a foster care proceeding, or in proceedings involving allegations of abuse or neglect.

Guardians ad litem for adults are most commonly appointed when there are allegations of incompetency, such as when a petition for guardianship or conservatorship is filed requesting that a guardian or conservator be appointed for an allegedly incapacitated adult.

The guardian ad litem meets with his or her client (the ward), explains the litigation to the client, meets with other parties or involved in the proceedings, attends all hearings, and often submits a written report to the court. The guardian ad litem acts as a factfinder for the court and bases his or her recommendations on what would be best for the client, and not on what the client wants. In other words, the guardian ad litem acts in the best interest of the minor or incapacitated client and does not take direction from the client.

Generally, guardians ad litem are regulated by state and local laws. Jurisdictions differ not only on when to appoint guardians ad litem, but also on the guardians' minimum qualifications, training, compensation, and duties.

FEES

The fees vary widely from state to state. In some states, the fees are very low, or capped at a low amount. In other states, such as Virginia, the rates are not entirely unreasonable ($55/hr for out of court work and $75/hr for court hearings) and are not capped (and you will even get paid for travel time, as well as a cost reimbursement of about fifty cents per mile). In some areas of Virginia (especially rural areas), it is possible to make a very decent living as a full-time guardian ad litem, working from home with low overhead. In other states, it is hardly worth your time monetarily, but the experience is invaluable.

In cases that are not paid by the state, which, in Virginia, includes most divorce cases and any guardianship/conservatorship cases with assets sufficient to cover an attorney's fee, you can charge your normal hourly rate of $100 to $300 per hour. Be sure that you will get paid before you agree to serve on these cases. The court will usually order that you get paid, but collecting the money may be bothersome, particularly in divorce cases. Try to get a retainer up front in divorces (usually the parties will split your fee).

WHAT THE PRACTICE LOOKS LIKE

Guardian ad litem for children

1. Get a phone call from the court (or an attorney in a private pay case such as a divorce) asking if you can serve on a case.
2. Receive the pleadings from the court.

3. Go to the courthouse and review the entire file.
4. Write to all parties and request a meeting.
5. Meet with your ward (perhaps in a home visit).
6. Meet with all other important parties.
7. Prepare a written report, if appropriate or if required by your court.
8. Attend the hearing, during which you may fully participate, introducing evidence, examining witnesses, and providing your recommendation to the court. Sometimes, all you will need to do is investigate and report.
9. When the case is over, submit your bill to the state or the parties.
10. Participate in any appeals.

Guardian ad litem for adults

1. Get a phone call from an attorney asking if you can serve on a case.
2. Receive the pleadings from the attorney.
3. Write to all parties and request a meeting.
4. Meet with your ward (perhaps in a home visit).
5. Meet with or talk to all other important parties.
6. Prepare a written report and file it in advance of the hearing, with a copy to all counsel involved in the case and any parties participating pro se.
7. Attend the hearing, during which you may fully participate, but in most cases you will mostly be providing your recommendation to the court.
8. When the case is over, submit your bill to the state or the appropriate party.

GOOD FIT?

This is a relatively low stress practice, but at the same time, you will acquire valuable courtroom experience. I found it to be the easiest way to ease into courtroom work, because you are always wearing the "white hat," representing the best interests of a person under a legal disability. You don't have to make any arguments that you don't believe in or support an agenda of a client with whom you disagree. Unlike other situations, you have the ability to meet with and talk to all parties prior to the hearing, so there is less chance of being "ambushed" by a surprise development. And, while you have the ability (and the responsibility) to fully engage in the litigation, there will be plenty of times when all you really have to do is investigate and report. And, since your opinion actually matters to the court, all parties are generally trying to be nice to you!

This is also a good opportunity to make a difference in the lives of children. Some of my most personally important and rewarding cases were those in which I was an aggressive guardian ad litem for a child that I believed needed my help. I feel that I made a big difference in the lives of many children, although there were also many sad cases in which I felt that there was nothing much I could do to change the tragic trajectory of their lives.

Being a guardian ad litem for children is an excellent way to learn the necessary skills to represent parents in custody and visitation cases. As a guardian ad litem in the courtroom, you will see many lawyers representing parents, and watch many doing it right, and many doing it ineffectively. You will see what works with the judges and what doesn't. It's a safe and easy way to get invaluable trial experience and get paid doing it. And if people like what they see, you will soon be getting calls from parents asking you to represent them.

If you do a good job in the courtroom, the local foster care agency may notice, and you could land a job working for your state's foster care program. The beauty of this track is that you may be eligible for the Public Service Loan Forgiveness Program, under which you can have your student loans forgiven after 10 years if you make 120 qualifying monthly payments while working for a qualifying employer. See my chapter on Public Service Loan Forgiveness for more information.

HOW TO ACQUIRE THE SKILLS

Virginia has a publication detailing exactly what is expected of a guardian ad litem for children, and it tells you nearly everything you need to know to get started:
http://www.courts.state.va.us/courtadmin/aoc/cip/programs/gal/children/gal_pe rformance_standards_children.pdf

The requirements for practicing as a guardian ad litem differ greatly from state to state, so you will have to go to your state bar website, as well as your court's website and/or clerk's office to find out what is required where you live.

In Virginia, a guardian ad litem must be a licensed lawyer, and you must take the qualifying course for Guardians ad Litem given by Virginia Continuing Legal

Education. Then, you must shadow a qualified GAL for two cases. Send all that proof to the state bar, and you are qualified as a GAL in Virginia. Then, you will appear on a list of qualified GALs for your jurisdiction, so the court or any attorney looking for a GAL can find you. You should also write to any courts you wish to practice in and let them know you are available, or they will probably not ever call you. Also visit the clerk's office and let them know that you wish to be on their call list. Courts tend to have their own local procedures for using guardians ad litem, so ask the clerk's office how it works in your jurisdiction.

You will also need E&O (malpractice) insurance.

PRACTICE FROM HOME?

I know lawyers who practice as full-time guardians ad litem from their home office. It works very well.

You will have to meet the child or incapacitated adult at their home, but that's good, because the court loves it when you do a home visit as part of your investigation.

HOW TO BUILD THE PRACTICE

_ Website not necessary.
_ Phone book: minimal listing only (white pages), so that people can find you if they look.
_ Become qualified and keep bugging the court's clerk's office until they call you.
_ Let local family law attorneys know you are available as a GAL for their cases, or, if acting as GAL for adults, contact lawyers who do guardianship and conservatorship cases and let them know you are available. It's always good to go in person and introduce yourself, so write a letter first, then follow up with a visit.

GUARDIANSHIP AND CONSERVATORSHIP

OVERVIEW

A Guardianship and a Conservatorship are what happens when an adult becomes incompetent or incapacitated and doesn't have an advance medical directive or a durable power of attorney giving someone the authority to make medical decisions on their behalf or conduct their personal business, should they become incompetent or incapacitated.

It is also done when an incompetent child (such as a child with Downs Syndrome) turns eighteen and becomes a legal (incompetent) adult.

A guardian is a person authorized by court order to make decisions regarding the physical body of another, such as making medical decisions, or placing the person in a residential facility such as a nursing home.

A conservator is a person authorized by court order to handle the personal affairs of another, such as his or her bank account, home, car, investments, and personal belongings.

Guardians and conservators have a fiduciary responsibility to act in the best interest of their wards. They are required to be bonded, and the conservator must file an annual accounting with the local commissioner of accounts.

WHAT IS INVOLVED?

Guardianship/conservatorship (let's just call them guardianships for short) are governed solely by statute. In Virginia, they are very easy. Just read the chapter in the code that talks about guardianships and follow its directions. It will tell you what the petition needs to say, who it needs to be mailed to or served on, what medical evidence is required, etc. It's very straightforward.

Uncontested guardianships are quick, easy, and low stress. In our jurisdiction, they are usually handled in the judge's chambers, rather than in open court, because they are so simple and routine. Contested guardianships, on the other hand, where family members are fighting over who gets control of Dad and his stuff, can be ugly and stressful. Fortunately, you can usually see those coming, and turn them down or refer them to a litigator if you don't want to do them.

Sometimes guardianships can be contested because the person who is the subject of the proceeding insists that he is not incompetent. Those can be pretty interesting, but it's mostly a matter of what the medical evidence says (and how your judge leans).

There are at least five ways to be involved in guardianship proceedings.

o   The usual way is to represent the petitioner. If it's uncontested and you have the proper medical evidence, you just jump through the statutory hoops, and it's done.

o   Sometimes more than one person wants to be the guardian, and the case is contested, and you are asked to represent a would-be guardian against the petitioner. This will be a full hearing in open court.

o   Sometimes the allegedly incompetent person asks you to represent them, to prove that they are competent. Again, a full hearing in open court, and an interesting position to be in.

o   If you are a Guardian ad Litem for adults, you might be appointed by the court to represent the best interests of the respondent (the allegedly incompetent adult). In this capacity, you investigate to be sure that your client really needs a guardian, that the person asking to be the guardian is the best choice, and that all of the proper procedures have been followed. See my chapter on Guardian ad Litem.

o   Another way to be involved is to actually serve as the guardian and/or conservator. In this scenario, someone else has filed a petition, maybe a nursing home or a family member who does not wish to serve as guardian but knows that one is needed. In Virginia, at least, a guardian/conservator is entitled to be compensated for his service, with a percentage of the assets, or $50 per month if the client is indigent (this usually comes out of social security or some other governmental subsidy). I know a couple of folks who act as guardian for a whole slew of unfortunate souls who didn't have anyone else willing to serve.

FEES

Uncontested guardianships usually bring fees of between $1,500 and $3,500, with ours averaging around $2,500. They are usually done on an hourly basis, although a flat fee is appropriate as well.

The fee for the Guardian ad Litem is charged by the hour, and may be close to $1,000 total, depending on the case. I've seen many higher and many lower. If the respondent is indigent, the fee will be paid by the state, and that rate varies considerably from state to state.

The cost of a contested guardianship is hard to predict, but they are usually done by the hour, and will usually cost at least $5,000.

The fee for serving as a guardian or conservator is determined by state law.

WHAT THE PRACTICE LOOKS LIKE

1. Get a phone call from a potential petitioner, whose loved one needs a guardianship and conservatorship. Schedule an appointment.
2. At the first appointment, use your intake forms to gather all necessary information. Quote a fee and receive your retainer, plus the filing fee for filing the petition (call the court ahead of time to find out how much.) Tell the client what to expect.
3. Obtain a medical report from the respondent's doctor (I write to the doctor and send an easy-to-complete form that contains all the statutory requirements. I also remind the doctor that the law allows me to obtain this report from him and that, if I don't get it in time for court, I will have no choice but to subpoena him to the hearing. Works every time.)
4. Call the court and find out what you need to do to schedule a guardianship hearing. This will vary from court to court. All I have to do in my rural area is call the judge's secretary, and I'll have several hearing date options immediately. In other areas, you may need to file a praecipe for a trial date. Ask the judge's scheduling secretary what the procedure is for your judge.
5. Advise your client of the court date and make sure they can be there.
6. Draft the petition, the order appointing guardian ad litem, and all notices as required by law.

7. Choose a guardian ad litem, if allowed to do so in your jurisdiction, or, if they are randomly chosen by the court, find out who it is, and call them to tell them about the case.
8. Follow up with the doctor until you get your medical report. You will need to file it in advance of the hearing.
9. Follow remaining statutory requirements (in Virginia we have to certify that we served everyone in accordance with law, etc.).
10. Prepare an order appointing a guardian and conservator in advance of the hearing, for the judge to review. He may also want to review your bill, if you are asking the respondent to reimburse your client. Make sure you send the order to the GAL in advance of the hearing for his or her review as well.
11. Prepare for and attend hearing with client.
12. Have final order entered. Get a certified copy for the client.
13. Walk the client through getting bonded and certified with the clerk's office.
14. Send a final bill to the client.

GOOD FIT?

Uncontested guardianships are a joy to handle. Since guardianship is a creature of statute, the laws and procedures are set out very clearly, and, unlike other types of courtroom work, with these cases you can enter the courtroom prepared and knowing what to expect. They are straight-forward, stress-free, and informal. (The contested ones can be quite a different story.)

This can be a natural segue into elder law. I started as a guardian ad litem for adults, then somehow the word got out that I was the "go to" person for guardianships, so I started getting a lot of calls from potential petitioners. Then, when I decided to enter elder law and Medicaid planning full force, I had a ready base of clients and referral sources for the elderly in need of nursing home care.

HOW TO ACQUIRE THE SKILLS

Find the chapter in your state code that deals with guardianship and conservatorship and read it. Make notes and checklists. Draft or obtain the necessary forms. If you can't find these in your jurisdiction, you might be able to find a closed guardianship file at your courthouse and get a copy of the forms used. In Virginia, there are a couple of fine attorneys who actually put their research and forms online for others to use, free of charge.

Look for seminars and publications on guardianship and conservatorship with your state's Continuing Legal Education providers.

Become a qualified Guardian ad Litem for adults. There may be a qualifying course in your state to teach you how to be a GAL for adults.

PRACTICE FROM HOME?

You can do guardianships and conservatorships from home, but you will need to find someplace to meet with clients, whether it is in their homes, or at the courthouse.

HOW TO BUILD THE PRACTICE

_ Website: a website will be helpful, because folks are searching online for lawyers. See my chapter on Websites.

_ Phone book: it's a good idea to be in the white pages and in the yellow pages, if you can swing it. Try to indicate in the yellow pages that you do guardianships and conservatorships. You might even call it Elder Law, because it's a type of elder law.

_ Newspaper: place at least an initial announcement when you start your practice.

_ Referral sources: Other lawyers can be good sources of referrals, if they don't do guardianships. Join your local bar association and introduce yourself at their next meeting. Let the whole bar know what kind of work you're looking for. You may also get to know the folks at Adult Protective Services, as they may want to refer people to you. The same is true for any local senior centers or local agencies on aging or Alzheimer's support groups. Another source of referrals would be groups dealing with disabled children who will turn 18 and become incompetent adults, such as children with Down 's syndrome or Autism. Nursing homes and retirement centers can also be referral sources.

- Education: giving talks about guardianships to church groups, or to groups dealing with Alzheimer's, Down's syndrome or Autism is a great way to generate business.
- Brochures and flyers are helpful, especially if you are giving talks to groups.
- Spread the word. Tell everyone you know, so that, when they hear of someone in need of a guardianship, they will think of you.

PERSONAL INJURY

OVERVIEW

The typical personal injury case arises out of a car accident, although a personal injury claim could arise out of any negligent or intentional tort causing injury. Some common types, besides motor vehicle accidents, are slip and fall cases and medical malpractice cases.

You may have noticed that there are many billboard ads for personal injury attorneys, especially in certain states, like Florida, where it seems like there's a personal injury attorney billboard on every block. The reason so many lawyers want PI cases is that they can be real money-makers.

WHAT IS INVOLVED?

Personal injury claims are usually aimed at collecting available insurance for an injury caused by the negligence of an insured. In auto accident cases, we are looking to collect against the defendant's liability insurer, either through settlement or lawsuit judgment. In medical malpractice cases, we are looking to collect from the doctor's malpractice insurer. In premises liability cases such as slip and fall, we are looking to collect from the landowner's liability insurer. Although the person whose negligence caused the injury is personally liable, we are not usually trying to collect from the defendant personally, but rather, will be satisfied with the available insurance proceeds, because it is much easier to collect.

Personal injury cases, once you know how to handle them, are not that hard. If, however, you have to go to trial (usually trial by jury), it becomes a different ballgame. Anybody can settle a PI case (assuming it's a decent case), but it takes some skill to be successful at jury trials. If the insurance company gets the feeling that you are afraid of trial, it will become very difficult for you to obtain favorable settlements. So, if you're going to take on PI cases, you have to either be ready to do battle in a jury trial (possibly against a very savvy and experienced defense attorney), OR you can co-counsel with an experienced litigator for the jury trial portion. Or else settle for unspectacular settlements for the duration of your career. If you have a good case and are willing to split the fee, you should be able to find someone willing to co-counsel on the jury trial. Or, if you want to be a litigator, choose an easy one to try to a jury to get the feel of it (client willing).

Slip and fall cases are a common type of personal injury case, although, in Virginia, at least, they are not easy to win. One must affirmatively prove that the negligent condition was known to the business or person in possession of the premises, and that they had a chance to remedy the condition but failed to do so. That kind of proof is usually hard to come by. In some states, the rules are different, and more favorable to the plaintiff. On top of that, Virginia is a strict contributory negligence state, meaning that any negligence on the part of the plaintiff completely bars recovery. Most states use comparative negligence, where the plaintiff's negligence may lessen the recovery, but not bar it altogether.

Medical malpractice is another ball of wax. In Virginia, and other states, there are slightly different rules applicable to medical malpractice cases, so you have to be sure not to run afoul of notice requirements or other quirky rules. To pursue a medical malpractice claim, you will need medical evidence, which means that you have to have a doctor who agrees with your view of the case, or who at least agrees that the defendant was negligent. This usually costs money. You will need to pay a doctor to review your client's medical records and give an opinion of whether or not there was malpractice. (Get that opinion orally, and not in writing, unless and until you know that it will be favorable to your client). This will cost probably a couple of thousand, depending on the type of doctor and his fee schedule. That money should come from the client. The doctor could say there was no negligence, and that's the end of that, unless you want to pay to try another expert. If the expert says there was negligence, then you get it in writing and move forward with a lawsuit and/or attempt at settlement. Trial costs a lot in medical malpractice cases, because you have to pay the medical experts to come to court. You also have to pay to take the deposition of the defendant's medical experts. Then you have a jury trial that is heavy in medical evidence. It's do-able, but technical, and a big deal.

FEES

Your fee is generally a contingency fee, and a percentage of the plaintiff's recovery, usually 33% (for example, for a $100,000 settlement, your fee will be $33,000), although some charge as low as 25%, and some as high as 40%. For medical malpractice cases, our firm routinely charges 40% because of the higher risk. If your client is a minor, the court will have to approve your fee, and many judges won't approve 40% on minors' settlements.

The client is responsible for all costs of pursuing the claim, including litigation costs.

WHAT THE PRACTICE LOOKS LIKE

1. Get a phone call from a person who was injured in a car accident. Schedule an appointment immediately. Ask caller to bring his own car insurance information.
2. Meet with client; make sure client was not at fault in the accident; get information about accident, defendant, and all insurance involved. Have client sign retainer agreement and sign medical releases to obtain medical records. Get information about all medical care received as result of accident. Instruct client to keep a journal and not talk to insurance company, etc. Review client's insurance for Medical payments coverage and UM/UIM coverage.
3. Make note of statute of limitations date and set several ticklers on your calendar. (In Virginia it is 2 years from date of accident.)
4. Write to police or state trooper for copy of accident report.
5. Find out defendant's court date for traffic charge and sit in on the hearing if you can.
6. Decide whether to help client with property damage claim, or just give him advice and let him proceed, and call you if he has questions.
7. Write to defendant's insurer to advise that you represent plaintiff.
8. Write to plaintiff's insurer, if Medical payments or UM/UIM coverage apply, and advise them that you represent plaintiff.
9. Write to all health care providers to obtain copies of medical records and medical bills related to accident. Keep track of all treatment and bills.

10. Determine if plaintiff has any liens against recovery, such as health care provider liens, ERISA lien, Medicaid, or Medicare. If any, write to lien holder requesting amount of lien.

11. If applicable, submit all medical bills and records to plaintiff's Medical Payments insurer for recovery. If the insurer refuses to pay in accordance with the contract, sue in lower court.

12. Follow plaintiff until he completes treatment or reaches maximum medical improvement, then discuss settlement with client.

13. Attempt settlement with liability insurer, by sending a long letter setting out the case and demanding settlement in a certain amount. If you can settle it, the insurer will send a check and a release. They will want to make sure you have taken care of any liens against recovery. Place the check in your escrow account, prepare a settlement disbursement sheet, and disburse to client, yourself, any lien holders, etc.

14. If no settlement is achieved, prepare lawsuit and file in appropriate court, requesting service on defendant and on UM/UIM carrier, if applicable.

15. Proceed with litigation if no settlement is possible. Conduct discovery (interrogatories, requests for admission, requests for production, depose defendant and defendant's expert witnesses).

16. Plaintiff and witnesses will also be deposed.

17. Set case for trial. Note all deadlines in court's scheduling order.

18. Subpoena witnesses, prepare jury instructions, etc.

19. Try case. Prepare final order.

GOOD FIT?

Personal injury cases, up to settlement, are a great fit for detail-oriented, organized types. Unfortunately, PI jury trials require the opposite type of personality: quick thinking orators who are good at debate and good under pressure. PI cases are done best when two lawyers work together: one who works the details and prepares the case for settlement or trial, and another who negotiates settlements and tries the case to a jury. It is also a good fit for a litigator with a very good paralegal.

Make no mistake, jury trials are very stressful. You could win big, but you could also lose completely, and get paid nothing for the months or years of work that led up to it. And your client has a lot riding on the outcome.

HOW TO ACQUIRE THE SKILLS

Unfortunately, personal injury is largely governed by case law, although the procedural aspects will be set out by statute. So, it is not as simple as just reading the statute and following it.

Fortunately, there are probably some good Continuing Legal Education offerings in your state, seminars and publications to teach you how to handle a personal injury case. Look for the, buy them, and study them.

Try to find out when a PI case is being tried to a jury in your jurisdiction, and sit in on the whole trial, from jury selection to verdict. That will be the best lesson you will ever receive. You could also review the court file and get a copy of the pleadings and jury instructions to keep as forms. If you talk to the clerk's office at your court, they will probably know when a PI case is going to be tried. Don't forget that the clerk and deputy clerks are your best friends.

In Virginia, there is a two-volume set of jury instructions that have been approved by the courts. You can buy them. I'm sure it's similar in your state. As long as you are using the approved instructions, you are golden. Actually, it's a great practice to look at the jury instructions first, when you are involved in a lawsuit, because they will tell you exactly what you will need to prove.

It's hard to jump into medical malpractice, but you can easily start by co-counseling with an experienced medical malpractice attorney on any clients you are able to obtain. They will usually be happy to work with you and split the fee.

For that matter, you can co-counsel any personal injury case with a more experienced attorney. The trick is to get the client. If you happen to get a good client with a good case, you will have no problem finding an experienced attorney willing to pursue the case with you as co-counsel for a share of the fee. Make sure the fee arrangement is ethically permitted under your state's rules.

PRACTICE FROM HOME?

This practice could theoretically be done from home. In fact, it is possible to handle a case entirely by phone and mail, up to trial preparation, although you will need a place to meet with clients (possibly at their home). However, at some point, you will want to have an office. It will give you more credibility.

HOW TO BUILD THE PRACTICE

_ Website: a good website is highly recommended.
_ Phone book: white pages and yellow pages are highly recommended, and try to make yourself look like a serious PI attorney in your yellow pages ad, if you can afford it. When you're just starting out, you may not be able to afford it. A lot of firms who specialize in PI take out a full page ad on the back of the phone book, which is not cheap, but it does provide a lot of exposure.
_ Referral sources: you can get referrals from other lawyers who don't do personal injury work, if they do not already have someone they like to refer to. The best referral sources will probably be your acquaintances and the churches, clubs, and community organizations you belong to. Spread the word and get your name out in your community.
_ Educating: offer to give talks or write articles about what to do if you're in an accident or feel you are the victim of medical malpractice.
_ Buy a share of advertising. There are numerous companies who advertise on television, radio, billboards, or internet, and refer the callers to any number of attorneys who subscribe to their service. You pay by the month. You will get calls. The caller may or may not be in your city or county – you can select the jurisdictions you will service. Some calls will be losers, some will be so-so, and every once in a while, they will be pretty good cases, or maybe even really good cases. It can be a good way to get your initial experience, if you are willing to pay the monthly fee for the opportunity. Google "Personal Injury Leads" to see some of the offerings.

REAL ESTATE TITLE SEARCHER

OVERVIEW

Perform real estate title searches for other lawyers or for title insurance companies. NOTE: This may be an area of work which is appropriate for those who are not yet licensed to practice law.

WHAT IS INVOLVED?

Nearly every sale of real estate, and every mortgage, requires that the title to the subject property be searched to verify that the current owner holds fee simple title, and to check for any liens that may have attached to the real estate, such as mortgages, judgment liens, and mechanics' liens. The search will also turn up any easements or other documents affecting the subject property.

The title search is done by searching the records in the "deed room," although those records are usually now online, at least back to a certain year, beyond which you will have to actually search the deed books. In Virginia, the deed room is the room in the Circuit Court court's clerk's office where the deed books live. Deed books are actual bound books containing copies of all deeds (and other recordable land records) which have been recorded since the inception of that courthouse. It is possible to search title through the deed books all the way back to land grants of large tracts from the government to private individuals. The older ones are hand-written and hand-copied, including the plats. After a certain year, they will be filed digitally, and you will be searching on a computer for a digital copy of deeds, plats, mortgages (or, in some states, deeds of trust), easements, boundary line agreements, etc.

You don't have to be a lawyer to search a real estate title, and most title searchers are not lawyers, but there is no harm in being a lawyer who searches titles. You will learn a lot about real estate, and you will be in a better position to trouble-shoot problematic titles and know how to handle them. I searched a lot of titles in my first job as a lawyer and feel that I learned a lot about real estate law from trouble-shooting difficult titles. Once you understand the titles and the issues involved, it is an easy jump into doing real estate closings, and, if you wish, real estate litigation, such as boundary line disputes or partitions of real property. You would also be in a good position to do tax sales, or sales of property for delinquent taxes, for local governments. (Sometimes the local government attorney does them, but sometimes the locality hires a lawyer who does nothing but tax sales throughout the state, because the sale tends to be handled more efficiently by a specialist.) Tax sales are not hard; you just have to be able to search titles, and read the statute governing how to do the tax sale procedure.

FEES

It varies. You could be paid a salary for full time work or be paid by the hour or by the title. Some titles are quick, and some can take many hours if you run into a snag such as a missing link in the chain of title, or a landowner who held many parcels, sometimes requiring lots of time to figure out which deeds pertained to your parcel.

Since this is work often done by a legal assistant or paralegal, you could expect legal assistant-level pay. Still, it's pay, and you're learning on the job and making valuable contacts with real estate lawyers.

NOTE that many jurisdictions routinely use title insurance companies to do their title searches, so it may be hard to compete in areas where this is the norm. More remote rural areas are often not served by title companies, and these areas may demonstrate a real need for title searchers.

WHAT THE PRACTICE LOOKS LIKE

1. Receive a file from your employer or receive a call from a real estate closing attorney who wants you to search a title. Get the necessary information to start (often a copy of the most recent deed, or the name of the owner and the property description).
2. Grab your title search forms, and either head to the courthouse or go online to begin searching the title.
3. Adverse the title to check the chain of title back 60 years or so; check for judgment liens and other liens; check to see that the real estate taxes have been paid; check for financing statements, if applicable. Write down all your findings and/or print out pertinent deeds, liens, plats, and information.
4. Provide the report to your employer.
5. Submit a bill to your employer.

GOOD FIT?

This is quiet and very low stress work. After several hundred of them, it can get right boring. If you're fascinated by history and real estate and like finding out how title passed through hands, you'll enjoy it.

If you want to pursue a career in real estate, this could be a good way to start out by getting paid to learn about real estate titles, deeds, mortgages, plats, judgments, and easements. You will get to know some real estate attorneys along the way. You will also get to know your way around the courthouse. Don't forget to be extremely nice to the clerks, as they can be your best friends, or your worst enemies.

HOW TO ACQUIRE THE SKILLS

Here is a course that offers to teach you title searching, with forms, for only $169: http://www.learntitlesearching.com.

You can also search your state Bar and your state's Continuing Legal Education providers to see if they offer a course, seminar, or publication on searching real estate titles.

In brief, it goes kind of like this:

1. Start with the name of the current landowner and some description or idea of the property you are searching, maybe the street address, or the acreage and locality. Look the owner's name up in the "land book" or tax assessment records. Write down the tax identification number of the property, and note the tax assessed value, and whether or not it is in "land use" for tax purposes. Sometime the tax land book contains a reference to the deed number.
2. Put together a chain of title:

    a. Look at the current deed (or find it in the computer). Note who conveyed the property to the current owner.
    b. Find the deed by which that prior owner got the property and see who conveyed it to them.
    c. Continue until you have a chain of title that goes back at least 60 years (or whatever the standard may be in your area).

3. "Adverse" each link in the chain of title, by searching the name of each person in the chain one at a time, and looking at all land record documents that pop up. Be sure to search not only the deeds and other land records, but also judgments (which constitute a lien on the property if docketed with the land records) and financing statements (which can be a lien on property fixtures). Get a copy of any records you find that pertain to your property.
4. If you find any mortgages, deeds of trust, or other liens, check to see whether they have been paid off and released.
5. If the property goes through a decedent's estate, you will make sure that the person who owned it next actually inherited it from the estate.
6. Go to the treasurer's office and check to see if the real estate taxes have been paid up to date. If not, get information about the delinquencies.

That is a very basic overview. There will be other details to know, but that's the basic idea.

PRACTICE FROM HOME?

This practice can definitely be done from home, although you will have to either search the deeds at the physical courthouse or pay a monthly fee for remote access to the records.

HOW TO BUILD THE PRACTICE

_ Website: not really necessary.
_ Phone book: not really necessary.
_ Referral sources: you may find work from real estate closing attorneys, real estate litigation attorneys, and title companies. In some jurisdictions, non-lawyers are allowed to close real estate transactions, so they may also use your services, although in many cases you will find that real estate closers, including lawyers, are accustomed to using title companies and not private title searchers. If you expand out into the rural areas, you may find places that title companies do not service. These are good areas of opportunity for you to find work with an attorney.
_ Join your local bar association and introduce yourself at their next meeting. Let the whole bar know what kind of work you're looking for.

SOCIAL SECURITY DISABILITY

OVERVIEW

You will be helping folks apply for social security disability benefits, usually with an administrative appeal after they have already applied on their own and been denied. NOTE: This may be an area of work for those who are not yet licensed to practice law, if your state allows non-lawyers to assist people with their social security disability claims.

WHAT IS INVOLVED?

You review the client's work history, health complaints, and medical records and compare them to the requirements for disability. If they don't have the evidence they need to qualify for disability, you either tell them they won't likely qualify, or, if you think they are sufficiently disabled but just need more evidence, you help them develop their evidence until they do qualify. If you can't get them qualified before the administrative hearing stage, you will appear with them for that hearing. If necessary, you will help them pursue further appeals.

As a broad overview, in order to be found disabled, an applicant must "meet or equal" a "listing" on social security's Medical Listing of Impairments. The listing tells exactly what medical findings are necessary to meet the listing. If your client doesn't have the necessary findings in their medical records yet, they may just need to return to the doctor for the appropriate evaluations.

Social security's regulations will tell you what is required to "equal" a listing, if you don't meet it exactly.

If the client doesn't meet or equal a listing, then you turn to the "GRID" rules to determine whether the applicant is disabled.

Every step of the way, you are comparing the client's reality to the requirements of the social security rules. Ultimately, you are hoping to persuade social security to declare your client disabled, and thus eligible for benefits.

FEES

The fee is set and capped by federal law. You will generally be entitled to 25% of the applicant's award of past-due benefits. (The award will be back-dated to the date of application, and it can take forever to actually get benefits – often a year or two, especially since you are generally representing those who were initially denied – so the back award can be substantial). There is a cap of $6,000 (at the time of this writing), so that is the maximum you can earn on any one case.

Be sure that your client is applying for SSD and not SSI. There is a good chance you won't get paid for SSI claims, since social security will not withhold your fee from the applicant's check, and thus the client will receive a check that includes your fee, and you must rely on the client to come back and pay you after they receive their award.

WHAT THE PRACTICE LOOKS LIKE

1. Get a phone call from a new client; set an appointment.
2. Meet with client, decide whether or not to take the case. Check the deadline on their letter from social security to be sure you have time to file an appeal. Check their work history to be sure they are eligible for SSD.
3. Have the client sign a medical release and a retainer agreement.
4. Write their medical providers to request medical records.
5. Go to the local social security office and ask to review the file.

6. Compare the client's medical records against the SSD legal requirements for disability.
7. Procure whatever medical evidence you may need and send it to SSD.
8. If necessary, prepare for and attend a hearing before an administrative law judge.
9. Wait for the decision.
10. Appeal further if necessary.

GOOD FIT?

This is a good fit for anyone with a medical background as an undergrad, but you don't have to have a medical background. It's not terribly difficult to compare the client's evidence to the SSD listings and GRID and determine what further evidence is needed. When in doubt, Google. Or, ask a doctor or nurse friend for guidance.

It helps to be detail oriented. Most of the practice will be studying medical records and regulations and figuring out how to make the two mesh.

It is a relatively low stress practice, although you may have to handle an appeal at the administrative law judge level or even the state court level.

It will take time to develop this practice and begin to have paychecks arriving in the mail.

If you think you might want to be an administrative law judge one day, this is a good way to gain experience towards that goal.

HOW TO ACQUIRE THE SKILLS

It's all statutory, so just read the law until you get it. Before you do, though, there are a lot of websites out there that will give you an overview and help you get started. For instance, here's a great explanation of how social security uses a grid system to determine disability:

http://www.nolo.com/legal-encyclopedia/how-social-security-uses-grid-medical-vocational-rules-decide-disability.html

Here are some helpful definitions:

http://www.ultimatedisabilityguide.com/social_security_definitions.html

Here's where to find the social security disability provisions in the Code of Federal Regulations:

https://www.ssa.gov/OP_Home/cfr20/404/404-0000.htm

Here is Social security's official Medical Listing of Impairments:

http://www.ultimatedisabilityguide.com/medical_listings.html

Read online overviews, read the rules and regulations, and find the necessary forms (most can be found either online or at your local social security office), and you are good to go.

PRACTICE FROM HOME?

You can do this type of work from home, but you will need to find a place to meet with the client. You could meet with them at your home office, at their home, or perhaps at a room in the courthouse, if your jurisdiction has a witness room or library that you can use.

HOW TO BUILD THE PRACTICE

_ Website: a website would be helpful, to capture people who are searching online for help with their SSD appeals. Having an active blog will help people to find you.

_ Phone book: I do recommend being in the white and yellow pages, if you can swing it. People still look there, believe it or not.

_ Newspaper: if you can run a cheap regular ad, it would be worthwhile. If nothing else, place an announcement when you begin your business.

_ Networking with referral sources: Other lawyers who do not do social security disability work are great referral sources. Introduce yourself and be sure to keep in contact with the most promising sources, so that you will be "top of mind" when they need to refer a client for SSD. Good choices are general practice lawyers, personal injury lawyers, bankruptcy lawyers, criminal and traffic defense lawyers, and family lawyers. Attend a local bar meeting and ask to introduce yourself and announce your new practice. Send letters to selected lawyers announcing your practice and follow up with a visit.

Churches and synagogues are also good sources of referrals. They might even let you leave brochures or flyers.
Doctors' offices are another good place for brochures, and doctors can be good referral sources as well.

_ Spread the word. Tell everyone in person, on Facebook, and on Twitter. Be sure to let local churches and community groups, and other lawyers know that you can help their folks.

TRAFFIC DEFENSE

OVERVIEW

Represent clients charged with traffic offenses, from speeding to reckless driving to DUI's and loss of license.

This is often carried out in conjunction with a criminal defense practice, but you could do either one separately.

WHAT IS INVOLVED?

You will advise clients charged with minor or serious traffic offenses, letting them know what kind of fines, loss of license, or even jail time to expect. You will need to acquire a feeling for your local judges and know what they are likely to do in any given situation. You will work frequently with the local prosecutors to try to obtain favorable plea bargains, where the client pleads guilty or "no contest" in exchange for a guaranteed outcome or sentence, whether that is having the case dropped after taking a driving course or going to jail for a reduced time for more egregious offenses.

FEES

The fees can range from a couple hundred dollars to several thousand dollars, depending on the seriousness of the case, and the standards in your local area. This can be a financially rewarding practice if you can get a high volume of business, since each case does not usually take a long time to resolve or try.

Some cases will need to be taken to a jury trial or an appeal, but the fee goes up substantially in those instances.

WHAT THE PRACTICE LOOKS LIKE

For most simple traffic matters, like a speeding charge, it goes like this:

1. Get a phone call from a new client charged with speeding. Get all pertinent information and answer the usual questions. Quote a fee and let the client know that you will not note as counsel with the court, or begin to represent them, until you receive the fee in full.
2. Receive the fee in full. Note as counsel with the court (write a letter to the court advising that you are representing the client in that matter). Note the hearing date on your calendar.
3. Tell the client to get a copy of his driving record for you, and, if applicable, tell the client to take a safe driving course and/or get his speedometer calibrated.
4. Talk to the prosecutor to determine if a favorable plea agreement can be achieved.
5. If the client likes the plea bargain, take it. Otherwise, decide whether the client needs to come to court and prepare him if necessary.
6. Appear in court to either enter a plea agreement or try the case (sometimes in the out-of-state client's absence).
7. Explain the outcome to the client. Follow up with a dispositional letter.
8. If the court takes the matter under advisement, with the charges to be dropped after a certain time if no other offenses occur, note the date and time of the review hearing, and make sure your client does whatever the judge told him to do by that date (such as take a safe driving course, etc.).

For more serious offenses, it looks more like this:

1. Get a phone call from a new client charged with reckless driving, DUI, or another serious charge. Get all pertinent information and answer the usual questions. Quote a fee and let the client know that you will not note as counsel with the court, or begin to represent them, until you receive the fee in full.

2. Receive the fee in full. Note as counsel with the court (write a letter to the court advising that you are representing the client in that matter). Note the hearing date on your calendar.
3. Tell the client to get a copy of his driving record for you, and, if applicable, tell the client to take a safe driving course and/or get his speedometer calibrated.
4. Review the court file and any evidence the prosecutor is required or willing to share with you (such as lab results, breathalyzer calibration records, video from the police car, etc.).
5. Evaluate the case for the necessity of any pretrial motions, such as a motion to suppress the evidence in the case of an illegal stop.
6. If a serious matter such as a DUI, evaluate the case for the necessity of an expert witness or jury trial.
7. Talk to the prosecutor to determine if a favorable plea agreement can be achieved.
8. File any pretrial motions, brief them if necessary, and argue them to the judge at a hearing.
9. Get your witnesses ready, if applicable. Prepare your client and witnesses for trial if applicable. Have your evidence ready.
10. Try the case.
11. Your court may require a separate sentencing hearing, if your client is convicted.
12. Explain the outcome to the client. Follow up with a dispositional letter.
13. Handle any sentencing issues. Your client may want to serve his jail time on weekends with work release, or in another jurisdiction, etc.
14. Appeal if necessary. (Obtain appeal fee first).

GOOD FIT?

This is just like criminal defense, only easier. If you'd rather talk than research and write, and you're not keen on details, you'll like this practice. Especially if you are good at thinking on your feet and coming up with creative arguments or responses. If you enjoy negotiation, even better.

These cases are over quickly. The turnover is fast, and each case generally does not drag on for long.

The simple traffic cases are very low stress. With the more serious charges, your client may have a lot on the line, including loss of license and jail time, and therefore it places more responsibility on your shoulders and creates a much higher stress level for you as well.

HOW TO ACQUIRE THE SKILLS

Each traffic charge is statutory, and so the statute that defines the offense will tell you exactly what the prosecutor will need to prove in order to convict. Your job is to know exactly what the prosecutor needs to prove, and look for defenses, weaknesses, deficiencies, or loopholes.

Technology provides defenses. The radar machine and the breathalyzer must be working properly, calibrated regularly, and used properly. The results of lab tests must be introduced properly into evidence, sometimes requiring the lab technician to appear at trial.

Expert witnesses provide defenses, especially in DUI cases. They can calculate the rate at which blood alcohol level raises and drops and how many drinks are required to achieve a certain level. They can raise a reasonable doubt about the results of a breathalyzer or blood alcohol test.

Constitutional challenges provide loopholes, particularly with regard to "the stop." You must learn all you can about when the police can legally stop a vehicle. If they didn't have the right to stop them in the first place, your client can skate. However, you should expect the police to be savvy about this and say something like "I witnessed the vehicle weaving within its lane." (My interpretation: "He was doing nothing I could legally stop him for, but I had a hunch he had just come from a bar. I maybe saw his car move slightly to the left while remaining within his proper lane of travel at all times.")

Most of the time, your client is just plain guilty, and you will be arguing that his great driving record and his important job (which requires him to have a driver's license and supports his five children), and his general good reputation, and maybe a reasonable excuse for not realizing how fast he was going because it was his brother's car, etc., are all good reasons for going easy on the guy. Besides, he's a veteran. And he was upset at the time because his wife got some bad medical news and there's no way he can raise the five kids without her.

Look for Continuing Legal Education offerings (seminars and publications) in your state regarding serious traffic cases. Try to find one that offers forms for discovery and motions.

Sit in on your local court's traffic docket and watch what happens. (Call the clerk's office or go online to find out what days your court hears traffic matters). Watch how evidence is introduced, and what objections are most commonly raised. Get to know your prosecutors and your judges. Get a feel for how it works, and for what a good plea bargain might look like. Find out what your judge is likely to do with someone driving 100mph (in our jurisdiction, they will get jail time), and what he or she is likely to do with someone speeding in a school zone. Get a feel for what a normal outcome is on a first DUI, a second DUI, and a third DUI. Spend a lot of time watching traffic court, until you start to feel like you can guess what the outcome will be. Then you will be ready.

If your state publishes a Judge's Deskbook, buy one or try to get your hands on one. (See if the local bar has a law library and look to see what books it contains). In Virginia, there is a Judge's Deskbook for Circuit Court (upper court), and a Judge's Deskbook for General District Court (lower court). These are invaluable. They are designed to be an easy reference for judges to use when they are unsure of the law. For instance, what are the exceptions to the hearsay rule? When can a police officer stop a car? Those kinds of answers are at your fingertips in these deskbooks.

If your state or your Continuing Education providers publish an evidence handbook, I'd advise getting one for anyone interested in doing litigation. Virginia has an excellent one, and it even comes in digital format. Keep this with you in court for those times when you are just stumped and don't know the evidentiary rule at hand. You will also refer to it often when preparing for trial.

PRACTICE FROM HOME?

You can do this practice from home, as many traffic matters can be handled completely over the phone until the day of trial, when you meet your client at the courthouse. You will need a place to meet with clients and witnesses for more serious traffic matters, however.

HOW TO BUILD THE PRACTICE

_ Website: a good website, with search optimization and a good mobile site are an absolute must. Our firm receives many calls from folks who got a speeding ticket just passing through our area, who are sitting on the side of the road using their phone to Google for a local traffic lawyer. Having a blog helps your search ratings.

_ Phone book: you should be in the white pages, and the yellow pages might glean you some business, if you advertise that you focus on traffic matters.

- Referral sources: Other lawyers who don't do traffic matters can make good referral sources.
- Educating: talking to groups gets your name out there as an expert in traffic matters. Offer to talk to groups and offer to write articles for newspapers or other publications on what to do if you're stopped by the police or charged with DUI.
- Direct mailing. In Virginia, we see a lot of direct mailing to potential traffic clients, and it appears to work. Some traffic lawyers routinely check the court's docket (or the docket of several courts in a geographical area) to get the names and addresses of people with new charges. They then send a form letter and business card to these folks, touting themselves as the best defense lawyer to call. Check with your state bar to be sure that it's allowed in your state, and also be sure that the language of the letter complies with your state's ethical standards for advertising by lawyers. There are also companies, such as http://www.arrestrecordmarketing.com who, for a fee per letter, will send letters out on your letterhead to all people charged under your chosen criminal statutes in your jurisdiction. These letters often produce clients.
- Spread the word. Tell everyone you know. Facebook. Twitter. Join and volunteer as much as you, to meet more people and let them know that traffic cases are your specialty.

QUICK STARTS

Here is a list of areas in which you can get started most quickly, getting paid to learn:

- **Guardian ad Litem for Children or Adults**
- **Court Appointed Criminal Defense**
- **Freelance Contract Attorney**

Other quick starts include

- **Collections**: just get one business to let you start collecting their debts. (This should not be hard, since you will be working on a contingency basis, getting paid a percentage of what you collect.)
- **Appellate work**: get one lawyer to let you help with his or her appeal.
- **Real Estate Title searcher**: get one lawyer to let you help with his or her real estate titles.
- **Conservation easements**: convince one landowner or farmer to let you assist with obtaining a conservation easement.
- **Traffic or Criminal defense**: contacting (by mail) persons recently charged with crimes or traffic offenses could land you your first client quickly.

OTHER AREAS

Here are a few other areas that I have not discussed in detail, but could be areas of practice for you to consider and explore:

BUSINESS FORMATION AND MANAGEMENT

Help businesses decide what type of entity to form and help them get formed and organized. Offer to be their "Registered Agent" for service of process while you're at it (we charge a low yearly fee for that service). The business will consider you to be their lawyer from then on and turn to you for their legal business needs.

CONSUMER PROTECTION LAW

Specialize in the federal consumer protection laws, about which most lawyers know very little. There are lots of folks out there who need this kind of help, and very few lawyers who know how to do it, including me. If you tackle this area of law, you should visit small law firms and solos and let them know that you are available to co-counsel these cases with them.

FORECLOSURES

Handle foreclosures for banks, and/or fight against foreclosure actions on behalf of landowners. You could find potential clients by watching the foreclosure notices in newspapers and on Zillow. Depending on your state's marketing ethics, you could possibly contact them by a letter detailing how you can help, and/or include a brochure about what you do. In our small firm, we are fairly regularly contacted by people seeking help with unfair foreclosure actions, who are trying to save their homes and can't succeed on their own.

LOCAL GOVERNMENT LAW

Represent local governments; attend their board meetings, help with the passage of local ordinances, represent them in controversies, etc. One good way to ease into this is to first learn to do tax sales (see below), then, when the government officials get to know you, offer to be their retained attorney. We generally charge a flat fee for this service, per month, with additional hourly fees for extra services, such as tax sales or litigation.

GOVERNMENT TAX SALES (REAL ESTATE)

Work for local governments and handle the sale of real estate for unpaid taxes. This is a statutory action, and not difficult to do, although there are numerous steps to follow.

PROBATE

Help families navigate the laws of probate when their loved one dies. Surprisingly few lawyers are knowledgeable at this, but it's a pretty easy niche to learn. Once you take the trouble to learn it, it can be an easy practice, and will lend itself well to having assistants do most of the work, although, on a budget, you can easily do this practice without a secretary.

REAL ESTATE CLOSINGS

Handle quick, usually easy real estate closings (spoiler alert: none of them go as planned.) Requires compliance with the Real Estate Settlement Agents Act (formerly known as CRESPA), including being bonded and having a separate escrow account for closing funds. This is a volume practice. The fees per transaction are fairly low, and this business works best when you do a lot of it. You can increase your fees by becoming a certified title agency, thereby receiving an additional fee per closing for the title insurance. This practice lends itself well to having assistants or paralegals do everything but the actual closing, which is attended by an attorney. In the beginning, you may need to do it all yourself.

See http://sandygadow.com/state-by-state-closing-guide/#VA and similar websites for information on each state's practice.

SCHOOL LAW

Specialize in the laws relating to students and schools. This is a very small niche about which most lawyers know absolutely nothing. Market yourself to general practice small firms and solos who have access to potential clients and would be willing to co-counsel.

WORKERS' COMPENSATION

Either represent companies or their insurers defending workers' compensation claims or represent the workers in their claims against the company's workers' compensation insurance carrier. Either way, it is a rather specialized niche, and it is best to pursue it as a specialty, especially on the plaintiff's side. Volume and structured processes help to produce a successful plaintiff's practice in this area. The fee per case is generally very low for the worker's attorney, although it's good hourly work for the employer's attorney. It's not cost-effective to just do a few of these cases every once in a while, so most lawyers refer these cases out, meaning that you can get referrals from other attorneys.

Made in United States
Troutdale, OR
12/04/2024

25758150R00087